Interacting With Audiences
Social Influences on the Production of Scientific Writing

T0347654

Rhetoric, Knowledge, and Society
A Series of Monographs
Edited by Charles Bazerman

Interacting With Audiences
Social Influences on the Production of Scientific Writing

Ann M. Blakeslee
Eastern Michigan University

Routledge
Taylor & Francis Group

LONDON AND NEW YORK

Copyright © 2001 by Lawrence Erlbaum Associates, Inc.
All rights reserved. No part of this book may be reproduced
in any form, by photostat, microfilm, retrieval system, or
any other means, without prior written permission of the
publisher.

First published by Lawrence Erlbaum Associates, Inc., Publishers

Transferred to digital printing 2010 by Routledge

Routledge

711 Third Avenue
New York, NY 10017

2 Park Square, Milton Park
Abingdon, Oxfordshire
OX14 4RN

Cover design by Kathryn Houghtaling Lacey

First issued in paperback 2014

Routledge is an imprint of the Taylor & Francis Group, an informa business

Library of Congress Cataloging-in-Publication Data

Blakeslee, Ann M.
Interacting with audiences : social influences on the
    production of scientific writing / Ann M. Blakeslee.
            p. cm.—(Rhetoric, knowledge, and society)
        Includes bibliographical references and index.
ISBN 978-0-805-82299-1 (hbk)
ISBN 978-0-415-76162-8 (pbk)
1. Communication in physics—Social aspects. 2. Technical
    writing. I. Title. II. Series.
QC5.3 .B53 2000
530'.01'4—dc21   00-039362
        CIP

To my parents
Mary and Jerome Blakeslee

Contents

Editor's Introduction

Charles Bazerman
University of California, Santa Barbara

Audience is central to rhetoric, for rhetoric is concerned with how words move an audience, influence their actions, persuade their judgment, change their minds. But because audience in rhetoric is typically treated as a projection of the rhetor's plan, audience has remained a shadowy concept. Audience tends to be considered as the rhetor can see it, or as the rhetor can address or invoke its possibilities, or as the text constructs subject positions for those who might hear or read the crafted utterance. The study of the actual response of real people to an utterance has been most often left to communication studies.

There are reasons for this tendency, for rhetoric serves primarily to focus and help realize the intentions of rhetors needing to act within rhetorical situations and with uncovering the intentions and techniques of already delivered utterances. Rhetoric circles more around the craft of utterance than around the concrete consequences of that utterance in the world. The concept of audience in rhetoric serves as a hortatory call to exercise the imagination—you need to imagine your audience, so you can speak to it; you need to imagine who that other rhetor was speaking to and how she was trying to move them to uncover her design. This hortatory imaginative invocation of audience does not immediately direct one to gain more concrete information about how audiences are affected by utterances.

Gaining concrete information about audiences, moreover, is hardly unproblematic. The audience is never stably nor absolutely and comprehensively knowable, nor knowable outside the attention-focusing effect of the utterance. The demographics of potential audiences will never predict accurately who will see and attend nor how much they will identify with other auditors to form a collective greater than an aggregate of individuals. Nor can the demographics predict how the utterance itself will gather or disperse attention, create unity or difference among potential auditors.

And with each moment the available participants and the conditions that constitute their potential audienceness change. Nor will the demographics of the present and attending auditors tell you what they feel and believe and perceive, for these are matters of individual sense-making, influenced by many factors, and driven by individual purposes in the moment. As a transitory social phenomenon that is separately and imaginatively constituted from each witness's position, the dynamic entity of audience affords no objective description. Finally, rhetorical analysis of audience tends to come at the wrong moment for capturing what one might be able to capture concretely about the auditors and their responses. Productive rhetoric must consider the audience before the delivery of the text (so the audience is in the uncertain future) and critical rhetoric is post-mortem, after the audience has dispersed.

So it does make a certain kind of sense simply to encourage the rhetor to gather as much as she can about the potential audience and develop her own perspective on how the utterance might influence them. "Do your best in the shifting world of human phenomenological orientation towards each other!" However, such a strategy, even if long experience with many audiences in many situations has given one a diverse and savvy rhetorical repertoire, still does not direct one toward knowing more about the concrete responses of the audience.

In practice, people find a practical solution to this dilemma, for rhetorical situations are rarely isolated events. Knowledge of audiences typically emerges from evolving sets of relationships and interactions rather than from disengaged descriptions. Over time, rhetors modify their behaviors, stances, and goals as part of their relationship with evolving audiences consisting of many speakers. Some specific elements of the audience's behavior in past circumstances may make certain typical aspects of their audienceness salient enough to evoke explicit comment that becomes sedimented into a generalization or advisory rule for approaching them.

This process of getting to know audiences through interaction is the news that Ann Blakeslee brings us about rhetoric from her sojourn among a team of physicists. In her ethnographic net, she has caught a team of physicists who need to know about new sets of audiences because they feel their work has interdisciplinary applications. They accurately see the fate of their innovation as dependent on how others utilize their ideas and techniques, but these audiences are a bit strange to them, unlike the audiences in their own specialty which they have learned about in their education, specialization, and professional life. So they have to learn about these new audiences, and this learning takes them down a path of interaction, adjustment, negotiation, and adaptation—extending to the point where one of the team goes as a postdoc to work in a lab in the target specialty.

The interdisciplinary character of the rhetorical problem these physicists face makes the problems and processes of coming to communicate with audiences more visible, but it turns out to be not so different than the process they went through to be socialized in their own discipline. Learning to communicate with one's peers is at the very core of learning to be a scientist, and is at the very core of making meaningful contributions, as Latour (1987), Myers (1990) and I (1988) suggested. Failures of forming relationships with readers are coincident with failures of meaningful vitality of erstwhile contributions. Successful contributions are the vehicles through which relationships with audiences are bonded.

Learning to interact with audiences, Blakeslee shows, is something that necessarily continues throughout the scientific career, for the making of knowledge is a social process of knowledge makers engaging others in what they believe they have found that is true, reliable, and useful. For knowledge lives only in the minds and practices of people, and in the artifacts that people make on the basis of that knowledge. Part of the fundamental challenge of those who would make knowledge is to find the means to plant that knowledge in the minds and lives of others, where that knowledge may find sustenance and continuing life. Blakeslee's physicists know that, although they may take shortcuts due to impatience with a troublesome project. By showing that there is no getting around the sociality of knowledge making, Blakeslee implies there is no solution but for scientists to keep interacting with audiences. That is the news Blakeslee brings us about science.

Preface

My study of the rhetorical practices of a group of physicists is aimed generally at understanding rhetorical processes in science and specifically at examining what these processes reveal about audience. I am essentially concerned with investigating how scientists learn about and then plan to persuade and influence their audiences. Most other studies of scientists' rhetorical practices have focused primarily on the scientists' finished or published texts. These studies have led to static conceptions of audience where authors, concerned with manipulating and dominating their audiences, make distant guesses about them based on assumptions and broad-stroke characterizations. However, looking at scientific rhetoric in actual interactive practice, which I do in this book, moves us beyond such text-based, intention-of-the-author views of audience.

Specifically, I report in this book on a study of the dynamic processes by which a group of scientists shaped, negotiated, and positioned a text within a specific community. In this study I examined the conversations and activities of a group of three condensed matter theoretical physicists as they situated and presented their ideas about Dynamically Optimized Monte Carlo (DOMC) in a paper addressed to an interdisciplinary community comprised of biologists, chemists, and physicists. I focused on these scientists' rhetorical activities and practices while composing this text over the course of almost a year. I documented and examined the complex social and rhetorical processes by which they learned about their audiences and presented their ideas to them.

My involvement with these physicists suggests an alternative view of audience based on cooperative interaction between authors and their interlocutors. In this view, real, functional knowledge of audiences comes only by entering into some community of practice, in which readers also become self-defining interlocutors and even participants in joint projects. Such processes also only occur slowly and over time.

More specifically, the approach that the three physicists took to learning about and addressing their constituents in multiple domains suggests that scientific audiences are complex, dynamic constructs that scientists learn about through ongoing interactions extending both throughout and beyond their work on a single project. Several of the physicists I interviewed for my study claimed that scientists begin this lifelong process of social engagement during their graduate training (see chaps. 3 and 6). At this time they gain initial exposure to their audiences by giving talks, attending conferences, and collaborating with their advisors. After graduate school, scientists continue engaging in these activities, which provide them with knowledge that they can draw on and use to address their audiences. For their part, the physicists in this study seemed to understand this dynamic conception of scientific audiences. They realized that they could not ignore or take for granted the ever-changing needs and concerns of their interlocutors, both those in the familiar community of physics, and those in the unfamiliar communities of biology and chemistry.

Here, I present a narrative account of how the physicists planned to address these unfamiliar communities and what happened as they carried out this plan. Chapter 2 addresses, in general, the rhetorical strategizing in which the physicists engaged to position their work. Chapter 3 describes some of the more specific approaches the physicists took to learn about their audiences. I consider in this chapter the differences in the physicists' approaches to learning about members of their own community versus learning about the members of the unfamiliar communities of biology and chemistry. I also identify some of the truncated and colonizing moves the physicists made in learning about their unfamiliar constituents. Such moves prompt us to think further about what audience knowledge really is.

In chapters 4 and 5, I follow the physicists' work into communal interactive dynamics, looking at their overt attempts to get feedback from members of their audiences, what that feedback was, and how they responded to it. These chapters, like the others, reveal the real and difficult issues of how authors get to know and speak to their audiences. Chapter 6 sets these issues against the typical training of graduate students into the rhetorical world of their fields, which I show to be a long, slow process of entering into a community of cooperative practice. Finally, chapter 7 sorts through various notions of collaboration and the distinctions made—along with the reasons for those distinctions—between authorial and audience roles.

This book is not a presentation of a general theory of scientific writing, but an investigation of the processes of getting to know and interact with audiences in real practice. By looking at scientific rhetoric in actual interactive practice, it is my hope that we can move beyond text-based views of rhetoric where authors use rhetorical strategies as aids in the manipulative control of audiences. In looking at the attempts of these three physicists to learn about and persuade their novel audiences, we can begin to acquire a more realistic sense of how scientific authors get to know and speak to their audiences. We can also begin to understand how scientific texts can successfully mediate interaction with audiences. Such insights will hopefully lead to a wider realm of inquiry into this important, but as yet little understood, issue of audience.

ACKNOWLEDGMENTS

There are many people to whom I owe a debt of gratitude for their help with this project. First and foremost are my research participants, Robert Swendsen, Djamal Bouzida, and Shankar Kumar, who so generously and patiently gave of their time throughout my project. I greatly admire these three physicists and wish that I could have offered or taught them even a small portion of what they taught me, about physics and about writing. I am also indebted to numerous other scientists who took time to talk with me about research and writing in science. I am especially grateful to Robert Kraemer and David Lazarus for teaching me so much about mentoring and publishing in physics.

In addition to the many scientists who helped with this project, numerous scholars in rhetoric also advised and mentored me and read drafts of my work. I am especially indebted to Chuck Bazerman for his tireless support, patience, and keen editorial eye. His vision of how this work could take shape, and the direction he offered throughout it, enabled me to develop and stay focused on my goals for the work. Numerous others also provided direction and support. Tom Huckin introduced me to Bob Swendsen and provided the early guidance that helped me to formulate my research questions and to begin analyzing and understanding scientific discourse. Dave Kaufer mentored me early on, exhibiting the same valuing of mentoring that Swendsen did. Elizabeth Donoghue-Colvin, one of my own graduate students, helped me prepare the index for the book. I am also grateful to Richard Young, Chris Neuwirth, Barbara Lazarus, Rich Enos, Sibylle Gruber, Marcia Dalbey, Cathy Fleischer, Nancy Allen, Russ Larson, and many others for their help, friendship, and support. And I owe special thanks to Dorothy Winsor, Barbara Mirel, and Michael Gaines for reading many early and later drafts of my work. Dorothy and Barbara provided invaluable insights and ideas that helped me re-vision the manuscript, and Michael offered that close, final reading that enabled me to make revisions when I could no longer see, myself, what needed to be done. I am also indebted to my editors at Lawrence Erlbaum Associates, Linda Bathgate and Nadine Simms. It was a real pleasure to work with such fine and talented editors.

Finally, I am indebted to my family and friends for their support and faith in me, and for their patience and humor, especially when my patience and humor failed me. I owe special thanks to my parents, Mary and Jerome Blakeslee; to my brother, John; and to Kim.

—Ann M. Blakeslee

1

Scientific Rhetoric in Interactive Practice: Physicists Getting to Know and Speak to Real Audiences

A physicist, Robert Swendsen, his graduate student, Djamal Bouzida, and a postdoctoral fellow, Shankar Kumar, saw an opportunity in their research to provide a useful and effective simulation tool for the members of their own field, as well as two other scientific fields. Aware of the difficulty of addressing and persuading their new audiences in these other fields, these three physicists used several strategies to analyze and try to dominate their readers, but also to gain information about and to understand these new constituents. They engaged in an energetic program of rhetorical strategizing through which they sought to learn about and even to obtain feedback from the scientists they were addressing with their work.

Looking at these scientists' attempts to get to know and speak to their unfamiliar constituents helps with exploring the conundrum of audience in science. In my research with these three physicists, I explored the question, "How do scientific authors get to know and interact with their audiences in real practice?" In investigating this question, I examined the audience complexities and problems the physicists encountered as they attempted to cross disciplinary boundaries with their research. I also examined the negotiations and tasks they engaged in as they planned to address these scientists. More specifically, I examined the process through which the physicists learned about their audiences, and the manner in which they negotiated meaning and persuasion among these heterogeneous groups. I also examined the dynamic process by which the physicists negotiated relationships, standings, identities, and expertise (with issues such as status, authority, and

1

experience at play) throughout the various stages of their work. My research allowed me to identify and sort out the social interactive processes that contribute to the formation of knowledge in science, especially in interdisciplinary contexts. Cross-field encounters like this one provide a productive research site for examining these kinds of issues. However, the issues at stake apply to all scientific communication—indeed, all communication—so my hope is that studies like mine will open up a wider realm of inquiry and help us to develop a more realistic sense of how authors and audiences interact in science.

CHALLENGING ACCEPTED PRACTICE: THE PHYSICISTS' RESEARCH AND THE RHETORICAL AND SCIENTIFIC SITUATIONS SURROUNDING IT

Swendsen, Bouzida, and Kumar, all condensed matter theoretical physicists, were concerned in their research with developing efficient methods to simulate biological molecules. They were testing a method called *Dynamically Optimized Monte Carlo* (DOMC), which is a flexible method that allows scientists to vary the parameters of the simulations. The physicists were finding that the DOMC method could simulate molecules more efficiently than another method, called *molecular dynamics* (MD), commonly used by biologists and chemists. In a 1980 article, two chemists, Northrup and McCammon, established the efficiency of the MD method and persuaded biologists and chemists to make MD their method of choice. Northrup and McCammon's work also suggested that the problem of developing efficient methods for performing biological simulations had been solved. Therefore, biologists and chemists, who for the most part accepted these scientists' claims, saw little need to research alternative methods.

The physicists, however, wished to determine if the DOMC method could simulate molecules more efficiently than MD and thus save on supercomputing time, a primary motivation for this kind of work. When they found that it could, they set about trying to persuade biologists and chemists to consider using the method. However, their attempts at carrying out this persuasion were complicated by several factors, not the least of which were biologists' and chemists' longstanding acceptance of MD. Another complicating factor was the physicists' status as outsiders to these communities—they were not well known by these scientists, nor did they have a reputation among them. Also, and no less significantly, the physicists' approach to and concerns in performing the simulations were very different from the approaches and concerns of the biologists and chemists.

As one example of these differences, Swendsen, Bouzida, and Kumar believed in applying these methods first to smaller molecules. They preferred this approach, they said, because smaller molecules do not strain computer resources and therefore provide more accurate readings of the efficiency of the methods. Biologists and chemists, on the other hand, preferred applying the methods right away to larger molecules because those are the molecules they are most interested in simulating. (I address the problems the physicists had with this approach in chap. 2.) This practice and biologists' and chemists' general preference for applications rather than methodological proofs became important factors in the physicists' eventual decision to publish the DOMC work in *Physical Review* (Bouzida, Kumar, & Swendsen, 1992). Although the physicists had originally intended to publish their findings in a biology or chemistry journal, they ended up publishing them in *Physical Review* after they received critical feedback on the paper addressing the work from scientists in these other fields. This study began when Swendsen, Bouzida, and Kumar were planning this paper, and this book follows the process they undertook from its initial stages through to the completion and submission of the paper to the journal.

STUDYING HOW THE PHYSICISTS LEARNED ABOUT AND ADDRESSED THEIR AUDIENCES

My research with the physicists, which took place at Carnegie Mellon University between January 1991 and January 1992[1], represents the first qualitative study of the composing processes of ordinary scientists, from jotting down planning notes to editing final text. It is one of the first and most substantial attempts to gain this kind of data and to follow a text into communal interactive dynamics. It is also the first focusing on situated cognition and learning in a scientific domain. Specifically, I look at the situated processes both by which the individual DOMC paper was composed and by which Bouzida, the graduate student in the group, learned to address and to become a member of his disciplinary community.

Although most rhetorical scholars have examined broad or global features of scientific genres and language, and changes in these features historically (e.g., Bazerman, 1988; Gross, 1990; Myers, 1990; Prelli, 1989), I focused in this research on the much smaller grain of a single rhetorical situation unfolding over a shorter period of time (1 year). I attended in my work not only to the products of that situation, but to the processes that created and led to those products. I examined finished texts, but added the dimension of planning and preparing those texts and all of the social and rhetorical activities (both formal and informal) that constitute everyday ordinary scientific practice, especially as it pertains to learning about and addressing audiences. Greg Myers supported such expansions in our investigations when he entertained the question of whether researchers need to go beyond texts to understand writing, or whether there is nothing beyond texts to which we can appeal. Myers (1996) contended that we must get out into the field and enter the flow of language and work. He added that we need to relate our findings, as well, to the larger social contexts for such work (pp. 605–606).

The Participants

My primary participant in this study, Robert Swendsen, completed his doctorate in physics at the University of Pennsylvania in 1971. For the next 2 years he worked as a postdoctoral fellow at the University of Cologne in Germany. He then spent 2 years at a research institute in Germany, 3 years at Brookhaven National Laboratory in New York, and 5 years at the IBM research lab in Zurich. In 1984, he accepted a position as professor of physics at Carnegie Mellon University.

At the time of my study, Swendsen had more than 80 publications. He began writing papers on applications of the Monte Carlo renormalization group in 1979, and he began using the Monte Carlo method to conduct simulations in 1986. His collaborations generally consist of himself and one or two graduate students and postdoctoral fellows. When I performed my study, he had advised three doctoral students and served on several thesis committees. For my study, I spoke with a number of graduate students in his department, and they characterized Swendsen as a competent teacher and a concerned advisor. Three of these students said they planned to ask Swendsen to advise them. Swendsen was one of four condensed matter theorists in his department; however, he was the only one who specialized in using the Monte Carlo methodology to perform simulations.

The second participant in the DOMC group, Djamal Bouzida, was 29 years old and nearing the end of 6 years of graduate work, the last 3 of which were under Swendsen's direction. Previously, Bouzida had worked with another advisor in electrical engineering. He left this project after 3 years when his fellowship funding ran out. At the time of my study, Bouzida was also writing his thesis and looking for postdoctoral positions (he eventually attained one in a biomedical engineering department at a state university in New England). Bouzida had been raised and educated in Algeria and his native language was French; however, he also spoke and wrote fluent English, which he had learned at a young age[2].

Finally, Shankar Kumar completed his doctorate in physics in 1990 at Carnegie Mellon. At the time of my study, Kumar held a postdoctoral position in the biology department at a neighboring state university. Although Swendsen was not his advisor, Kumar had worked with Swendsen on the DOMC project, which resulted in Kumar's first publication. Kumar, who was 31 years old when I conducted my study, was a nonnative speaker, but he could write and speak English fluently: He had been educated in English-speaking schools in India, and he had lived in the United States for 8 years.

Sources of Data

In carrying out my study of these scientists, I relied on three primary sources of data—observation of group meetings, text analyses, and interviews (see the table in the appendix at the end of this chapter for a summary of the primary data I collected over the course of my study). I used these sources of data to develop a composite portrait of the interactions that occurred among these physicists and between the physicists and other scientists (i.e., those who read and responded to a draft of the DOMC paper and those who attended colloquia at which the physicists discussed their work). I focused my investigation on the interactions of the physicists (among themselves and with members of their audiences) as they worked out their rhetorical strategies and as they wrote and reviewed drafts of the DOMC paper (the physicists produced and jointly reviewed 21 distinct versions of this paper over a 5-month period).

I used the physicists' group meetings, which occurred once or twice each week and lasted up to 2 hours, as the primary source for my observations of their interactions. I also occasionally observed the physicists interacting informally with each other and with other scientists, either in one another's offices, in the hallway, or at weekly lunchtime forums; however, I did not record or formally analyze these exchanges. Although some organizational and social researchers have addressed the importance of such ad hoc, informal exchanges, I believed that all of my data sources, taken together, along with my frequent interactions with the physicists and immersion in the activities of their collaboration over the course of my study, provided sufficient data and information for answering the questions I had posed about the physicists' rhetorical practices.

During my study with the physicists I observed, took notes on, and tape-recorded 13 meetings at which they reviewed drafts of the DOMC paper, usually paragraph by paragraph. I also observed and tape-recorded 15 meetings at which the physicists discussed other aspects of their work and/or reviewed drafts of another paper they were writing that addressed multiple histograms. (Although I considered these meetings when I analyzed my data, they do not figure as prominently in my analyses because I was concerned in my study, primarily, with the strategies the physicists used to position their claims for the DOMC method in the fields of biology and chemistry.) My notes on the discussions that occurred at all of the meetings I attended totaled 249 double-spaced pages. I used the tapes as backup to my notes.

At the physicists' meetings, Swendsen usually led the discussions by addressing the revisions that he felt were needed in the drafts. In response to Swendsen's feedback at these meetings, Bouzida and Kumar produced and distributed new, full-text drafts that Swendsen would review prior to the next meeting (Bouzida and Kumar produced drafts of the DOMC and multiple histogram papers, respectively). My analyses of these drafts served as an additional source of data and complemented my observations of the meetings. In these analyses I compared current and previous drafts and documented all changes the physicists made from one draft to the next. I also referenced my meeting and interview notes to determine apparent reasons for the changes (or lack of changes)[3]. I analyzed 8 drafts of a conference paper on DOMC that the physicists had written previously, 19 drafts of the multiple histogram paper, and 22 drafts of the DOMC paper—an unusually high number, according to Swendsen, who said the number of drafts for this paper resulted from the group's unfamiliarity with their interdisciplinary audience.[4]

The distribution of work in the physicists' collaboration and the allocation of authority through control of revisions generally occurred in the same manner throughout my study. Bouzida and Kumar wrote the drafts of the papers, and Swendsen reviewed and responded to them and guided the revisions—he essentially led the discussions on the merits of Bouzida's and Kumar's writing and exercised the authority to accept or reject the drafts. Bouzida and Kumar, for their parts, revised and rewrote the drafts, with only one exception—Swendsen completely rewrote the third draft of the DOMC paper without any input from Bouzida or Kumar (see chap. 6). He did this because Bouzida was having difficulties with the early drafts, and these difficulties had started to frustrate Swendsen. He essentially wanted to expedite the process, and he exercised his authority as Bouzida's advisor and as the leader of the collaboration to do this.

Finally, in addition to attending the group meetings, analyzing all of the drafts and papers the physicists produced, and observing their general patterns of interaction, I conducted a number of informal interviews with the participants (lasting up to 1 hour). I requested such interviews when I wanted the subjects to elaborate on changes in the text or exchanges in the meetings. For example, I interviewed Bouzida and Kumar in order to understand their reasons for making or not making the various changes Swendsen requested in the texts. I was also interested in differentiating when their actions resulted from their agreeing with Swendsen's suggestions and when they resulted from other factors, such as their beliefs that certain changes were necessary or unnecessary. I also interviewed Swendsen periodically to elicit his responses to Bouzida's and Kumar's actions and progress on the drafts. I wrote out questions for all of these interviews, but I generally used them only as starting points, preferring that my subjects lead the discussions. I intervened in these discussions only as necessary to prompt elaboration. When the project was completed, I had conducted 8 interviews with Bouzida, resulting in 38 double-spaced pages of notes; 7 interviews with Kumar, for a total of 26 pages of notes; and 12 interviews with Swendsen, resulting in 49 pages of notes.

I also conducted informal interviews with 2 physicists outside of the group, once every 2 to 3 weeks throughout the study, to obtain their perspectives on the physicists' actions, to seek elaboration of issues raised by my study, and to verify my interpretations.[5] One of these physicists (identified in this text by the pseudonym Steve) was an experimentalist in condensed matter physics who had worked on problems similar to those with which the physicists were engaged. Because this physicist was on Bouzida's thesis committee, he was familiar with the group's work. The other physicist (identified by the pseudonym Bob) was an experimentalist in high energy physics and was unfamiliar with Swendsen's work (he conducts his own work at the Cern particle accelerator in Switzerland in collaboration with more than 200 physicists). I interviewed this physicist, and four others with different specializations (identified by the pseudonyms Rich, Brad, Len, & Eric), although less frequently, to determine if what I was seeing occurs in other areas of physics. I also interviewed a biophysicist and a chemist (identified by the pseudonyms David and George, respectively) who read and responded to a later draft of the DOMC paper, and whose responses led the physicists to alter the text and to change their plans for publishing and positioning the work.

RHETORICAL CONCEPTIONS OF SCIENTIFIC AUDIENCES

In the past two decades, scholarly work has shown the seminal role of rhetoric in the construction of scientific knowledge. We now know much more than we did about the rhetorical features of scientific discourse, especially of major scientific genres such as grant proposals and journal articles. We also know, intuitively if not empirically, that rhetoric permeates many, if not all, aspects of scientific activity, and that it plays an important role in the perpetuation and reproduction of scientific practice and social life. Echoing these presumptions, Latour and Woolgar (1986) said that scientists are basically "writers and readers in the business of being convinced and convincing others" that their statements should be accepted as facts (p. 88). They also noted that scientific discourse has no privileged status but relies instead on rhetorical and persuasive devices (p. 184).

Charney (1993) similarly said, "the aim of scientific discourse is profoundly argumentative and not merely expository; the goal is to persuade readers, to convince them of the validity and importance of the work, and to motivate them to acknowledge the force of the contribution by explicitly accepting and building upon it" (p. 204). Bazerman (1988) likewise argued that persuasion is at the heart of science. He said, "the most serious scientific communication is not that which disowns persuasion, but which persuades in the deepest, most compelling manner, thereby sweeping aside more superficial arguments" (p. 321). Even the scientists who formed the Committee on the Conduct of Science of the National Academy of Sciences, in their report *On Being a Scientist* (1989), portrayed scientific activity as inherently contingent and rhetorical rather than as epistemologically privileged.

However, despite these claims about the persuasive nature of science, and the general belief that scientific work cannot be accomplished without rhetoric, much previous work in rhetoric that has addressed science has tended to assign a very small role to the important rhetorical notion of audience. A good example of this is Perelman and Olbrechts-Tyteca's (1969) treatment of scientific audiences in *The New Rhetoric*. These scholars, in explicating their theory of the new rhetoric, which otherwise highlights the importance of audience, contended that "the scientist addresses himself to certain particularly qualified men, who accept the data of a well-defined system consisting of the science in which they are specialists" (p. 34). A scientist, in their view, can take for granted that all members of the audience, because they have the same training, qualifications, and information, will reach the same conclusions (p. 34). In addition, the scientific institution, in general, links scientists with their audience and eliminates the need for scientists to be overly concerned with audience (p. 18). They said,

> It is true that these authors when addressing a learned society, or publishing an article in a specialized journal, can afford to neglect the means of entering into contact with the public, for the indispensable link between the speaker and audience is provided by a scientific institution, the society, or the journal. In such a case, then, the author has merely to maintain, between himself and the public, the contact already established by the scientific institution. (p. 18)

Bitzer and Kinneavy, who wrote around the same time as Perelman and Olbrechts-Tyteca, similarly distinguished scientific discourse from other rhetorical discourses on the basis of classical conceptions of science and rhetoric—science is founded on truth and is therefore distinct from persuasion. Bitzer (1968) said, "The scientist can produce a discourse expressive or generative of knowledge without engaging another mind" (p. 8). Kinneavy (1971) made similar claims in his treatment of referential discourse in *A Theory of Discourse*.

Unfortunately, these views of scientific audience are not exclusive to these earlier rhetorical works. Even more recent works in the rhetoric of science support a view of rhetoric as a construct of the author to aid in manipulative control of audiences. The prevalence of such views is perhaps not surprising because scholars in this area have tended to focus on the strategic thinking of writers on the verge of utterance and because their studies are based mostly on analyses of finished texts.[6] However, unlike the earlier rhetoricians, and to their credit, these scholars also articulated an awareness of the importance of interactive dynamics, and some even advocated examining these dynamics empirically. I next review five significant book-length works in this area to show how they both address and reveal these various views.

In the first major and still seminal book in the field, *Shaping Written Knowledge: The Genre and Activity of the Experimental Article in Science* (1988), Bazerman emphasized, but did not study through an empirical examination of developing texts, the scientific process. He addressed this process, which certainly encompasses audience, by saying:

> Because the final text is so dependent on the process by which it is produced, it is important to consider how you should go about producing the text so as to wind up with the kind of statement you hope for.... In fact, process is so important to the production of persuasive scientific arguments that the final representation or writing-up seems a limited activity, with all the major parameters of the text determined by prior decisions. Well-considered procedure is not only good science, it results in good rhetoric. (p. 328)

However, he primarily analyzed already existing statements in finished and, in most cases, historically significant scientific texts. Traweek (1992) critiqued Bazerman's work by noting that his history of the rhetorical strategies used in scientific writing is not enough. Turning Bazerman's own observations back to him, she said we also need to consider how these strategies are informed by and, in turn, inform daily practice.

In another important work in this field, *A Rhetoric of Science: Inventing Scientific Discourse*, Prelli (1989) also relied on scientists' finished texts for his analyses. Prelli, who is concerned with scientists' inventive strategies, argued that the invention of scientific discourse is guided by certain prescribed logical/rhetorical (normative) principles. These general principles, he claimed, guide scientists' inventional decisions regardless of the community, or audience, being addressed[7]: There are identifiable lines of thought used repeatedly in the sciences and these lines of thought legitimize scientific observations and claims because they derive from what is accepted and valued in scientific communities; they aid scientists in deciding what to say and how to say it (p. 216).

Prelli's views perpetuate a domination-of-the-audience view of rhetoric. In Prelli's conception, scientific specialties (and hence audiences) are generally homogeneous: They have constituents who possess similar values and communally shared standards of reasonableness (pp. 112–113). The inventional principles that guide the creative and evaluative processes of scientific argument can therefore be delineated, and choosing what to say is a systematic enterprise (p. 118). Thus, although Prelli's is a seminal work on scientific topoi and stasis, it is also an incomplete picture—one that suggests the fixed and systematic qualities of rhetorical activities like invention instead of addressing how scientists' inventional choices may also be situational.

Another important work in the rhetoric of science, Gross's *The Rhetoric of Science: The Rhetorical Analysis of Scientific Texts* (1990), seemed to go a bit further in acknowledging interactions and the social character of scientific knowledge. Gross viewed science as a rhetorical enterprise centered on persuasion (p. 49). He also viewed science as a product of human interactions, and he argued that scientific knowledge is social and the result of persuasion (p. 20). He said that a rhetoric of science is thus concerned with studying persuasive structures in the sciences (p. 49). In addition, Gross argued that just looking at scientific texts in isolation is insufficient and that investigators need to examine the earlier stages of the complex persuasive process by which new science passes from private to public (p. 129).

However, for Gross these earlier stages encompass the peer review process and not the planning and composing processes that precede it (p. 129). In addition, rather than examining in his work the ways in which strategies, courses of action, textual choices, false starts, dead ends, and reconceptions of plans and goals incrementally shape texts and forums, often in unpredictable ways, Gross inferred only one seeming set path to finished texts from already positioned and established works. He focused, like Prelli and Bazerman, on finished and historically significant scientific works rather than examining the processes by which scientists employ these various rhetorical tools and strategies in the works that they are planning or currently developing. Gross also portrayed scientific audiences primarily in abstract terms. He addressed how "all scientists attribute to imagined colleagues standards of judgment presumed to be universal ... in the sense that anyone, having undergone scientific training, must presuppose them as a matter of course" (pp. 18–19).

Myers and Winsor made somewhat larger strides in moving beyond such text- and intention-of-the-author views of scientific rhetoric. Myers (1990), in *Writing Biology: Texts in the Social Construction of Scientific Knowledge*, captured the dynamics that occur during the planning and preparation of scientific papers. Myers viewed texts as structures for thinking and social interaction; he viewed them as a means for investigating social negotiations in science. In fact, he even criticized traditional literary, sociological, and historical analyses of scientific texts for not addressing the dynamic relation between knowledge and its textual representation (p. 8).

Winsor, the author of *Writing Like an Engineer: A Rhetorical Education* (1996), said scholars investigating the rhetoric of science and technology are engaged in a joint endeavor of understanding how specialists construct knowledge in their fields. Winsor corroborated Myers when she said, "Knowledge is formed in interpersonal negotiation over interpretations of evidence rather than simply in the close individual examination of an unambiguous reality" (p. 5). She likewise viewed language as the means by which practitioners in a field create knowledge and said that knowledge is created in an interplay of physical reality and knowers and in persuasive interaction among knowers (p. 69). She viewed persuasion as interactive, multidirectional, and ongoing (p. 70).

Myers shared these viewpoints. He employed literary and discourse analytic techniques in his work to examine scientific proposals, journal articles, and scientific popularizations; he examined the choices authors make in composing these documents, along with the reasons for these choices. Myers also analyzed the changes that the scientists in his study made in response to the feedback they received from reviewers and editors. By documenting and examining such processes, Myers elucidated important aspects of scientific rhetorical practice. He was also one of the first rhetorical scholars to include in his work the reactions and thoughts of the authors whose texts he examined.

Although Myers took these important additional steps, he also still relied primarily on finished texts for his analyses. He justified this focus by citing the practical benefits of texts: They hold still and are portable; thus, he can do things with texts that he cannot do with other kinds of data (pp. 6–7). Because of his focus on finished texts, Myers did not fully examine in his work the processes by which scientists conceptualize, develop, and write down their ideas; he focused, instead, on how they modify and renegotiate those ideas, which were already formulated in his work, based on the fairly formal feedback they receive from reviewers. His analysis thus also excluded many of the important earlier stages of rhetorical activity in science. Despite these limitations, Myers's work was a very important precursor to my own. By looking at scientific rhetoric in actual interactive practice, as Myers did, and as I did in my study, we can move beyond intention-of-the-author, manipulation-of-the-audience views of rhetoric to understand how scientific texts can successfully mediate interactions.

WHAT A STUDY OF SCIENTIFIC RHETORIC IN INTERACTIVE PRACTICE REVEALS

The findings from my research with the physicists suggest several conclusions regarding audience and interactive practice in science. First, distant guesses about audience based on assumptions about uniformity or broad-stroke characterizations aimed at manipulation and domination rather than cooperative interaction do not work very well. Intimate, interactive knowledge of audiences pushes authors to stronger, more effective arguments. Second, real functional knowledge of audience comes only over time by entering into some community of practice in which readers become self-defining interlocutors and joint projects emerge.

To persuade and gain adherence and support for their ideas, scientists must determine how to target and appeal to their audiences. My investigation reveals that the physicists used a number of strategies to identify and reach the audiences they were targeting, especially those that were new and unfamiliar to them. In chapter 2, I show the energetic project of rhetorical strategizing and gaining feedback by which the physicists identified and addressed their audiences and positioned their work in relation to their own field and the unfamiliar fields of biology and chemistry.

Chapter 3 addresses some of the specific strategies the physicists used to learn about these various constituents. I focus in this chapter on the process by which the physicists got to know and interact with their audiences in real practice. My findings reveal the messiness and trade-offs entailed in understanding and persuading audiences from different communities of practice. Looking at how the physicists tried to cope with a limited amount of information about their audiences provides a perspective on the real and difficult issues of how one gets to know and speak to an audience. The physicists' actions, in this instance, suggest a model of ongoing social interaction that is at times qualified as authors make trade-offs because of both time and other constraints.

Chapters 4 and 5 follow the physicists' DOMC text into communal interactive dynamics. I show the physicists coming to know and being influenced by their audiences on a direct and personal level. These chapters show, up close, the processes of getting to know and interacting with audiences in real practice. I look at the physicists' overt attempts to get feedback from members of their audiences, what that feedback was, and how they reacted to it. My findings in these chapters provide a realistic and concrete sense of how authors may interact with audiences and what results from that interaction. I also show all of this to be a gradual, limited process.

Specifically, looking at the physicists' interactions with these scientists reveals the negotiations, uncertainties, disagreements, and messiness that occurred as the physicists interacted with these members of their audiences. My up-close examination of these interactions reveals how they impacted the physicists' composing activities more generally, as well as how the interactions influenced the physicists' revisions to the DOMC paper more particularly. I show how the physicists responded to their readers' objections by clarifying their purpose for the paper and by trying to argue against the objections. The more they learned about these audiences, the more they distinguished their own position, the more forcefully they articulated it, and the more they identified the differences between their own beliefs and those of their audiences. The physicists also essentially gave up attempting to communicate with the audiences they found too difficult. They switched their audience to other physicists who would be more receptive from the start because they viewed the work from a similar perspective.

The whole idea behind having Bouzida write the DOMC drafts was to help him to learn how to write a scientific research article. An important part of that is learning how to address and adapt one's writing to audiences, which in this case was made more complex by the audiences being unfamiliar even to Swendsen. Chapter 6, therefore, addresses how Bouzida got to know and learn to speak to the audiences for the DOMC work. In it I show parts of a long, slow process of entering into a field of cooperative practice. I look at the training of Bouzida into the rhetorical world of his own field—how he got to know and speak to the audiences of his own field, as well as these other fields. I essentially look at the apprenticelike process by which a newcomer acquires audience and rhetorical knowledge. I examine the dynamic interplay and interactions that occurred between Swendsen and Bouzida as they composed the DOMC paper.

My findings with regard to students' acquisition of rhetorical skills share many similarities with Winsor (1996), who studied this process of disciplinary socialization in engineering. Winsor likewise emphasized the importance in learning of engagement in authentic language practices and in the practices of a profession (p. 8). She talked about the socialization of engineers occurring, as with the physicists, through their interactions with experienced engineers and through exposure to the texts those engineers produce (p. 19). She also captured the ongoing need for and nature of socialization, which encompasses both of the senses in which I also examine it—the socialization of newcomers as well as that of more experienced members of a domain who must keep up with the domain and/or who seek to enter new domains (see chap. 3 for a consideration of the latter). She said:

> The process by which the students are establishing themselves as engineers appears to be ongoing, suggesting that it may need to be continually engaged in as the engineer moves through various local contexts. That is, a person's identity as a competent member of a disciplinary community is something that may need to be continuously achieved, and thus as something that continuously varies depending on local conditions. Moreover, what constitutes competency might be expected to vary at different points in any career.... Finally, the activity system known as engineering is itself always changing, meaning that what counts as expertise changes too. (p. 106)

Such changes were certainly issues for the physicists as they engaged in the DOMC work.

Finally, chapter 7 reviews and summarizes the interactions that contributed to the formation of knowledge in this case. In this final chapter, I reconsider the multiple interactive processes that occurred as the physicists produced and publicly positioned the DOMC paper. I present both Swendsen's and my own perspectives on authorial and various other roles in scientific work, including various audience roles, and on how they influence the formation of knowledge in science. Understanding audience and other roles, and the influence they have on emergent statements, serves several purposes: It allows us to expand our views outward from the narrower notion of collaboration to the broader notion of social interactive processes that influence knowledge formation; it extends our understanding of how such processes operate in, influence, and help to structure science and scientific knowledge; and it allows us to identify, label, and draw finer distinctions between these interactive processes, helping us, in turn, to better understand the effects that these processes, which encompass audience, may have on scientific practice.

CONCLUSION

Generally, what I found in my study of how the physicists learned about and addressed their audiences for the DOMC work is that Swendsen, Bouzida, and Kumar acted rhetorically with intention and thought but in a manner that seemed part of the ordinary operations of science. Knorr (1979) noted with respect to scientists opportunistically tinkering in the lab, "Scientific [and rhetorical] activities can ... be seen as a progressive *selection* of *what works* by using what *has worked* in the past and what *is likely to work* under the present, idiosyncratic circumstances" (p. 369). She added, "The constructions obtained do not result from necessity: the *same* problems tackled in a tinkering process are likely to lead to outcomes which *differ* according to the idiosyncrasies of their production" (p. 369). Recasting this in rhetorical terms, one could say that the same or similar rhetorical situations are likely to lead to different rhetorical actions and outcomes depending on the idiosyncrasies of those situations (such as new and unfamiliar audiences). In this study I found Swendsen, Bouzida, and Kumar responsive to the contingencies of audience, making local, improvisatory rhetorical decisions that ultimately impacted the shape of their work and who it reached.

My analyses throughout this book reveal the numerous fronts, trials, manipulations of genres, and rhetorical appeals the physicists used as they engaged in this strategic enterprise of addressing different disciplines. Such an enterprise suggests that there is no right or wrong way to act in such situations; there are, instead, better or worse ways of acting, which are tied to circumstances. Furthermore, the rhetorical actions that scientific authors choose become starting points for subsequent moves and inquiries. And finally, the fine-grain level of detail revealed by my study shows that scientific audiences are complex and dynamic entities that require strategic, lifelong learning rather than one-time mastery.

Appendix A

Summary of Primary Data Sources

DOMC Drafts (date, page breakdown[a])	Review Meetings (date, pages of notes, transcript lines per participant[b])	DOMC Draft Analyses (pages, noteworthy changes or shifts in drafts)	Interviews (date, pages of notes, subjects discussed)	
			Bouzida	Swendsen
1 3/5/91 25 pp. total 16 pp. text 1 p. references 8 pp. figures	3/5/91 8 pp. Swendsen, 95 lines Bouzida, 13 lines Kumar, 13 lines	11 pp.	3/7/91 9 pp. On initial draft and its reception	None
2 3/8/91 13 pp. total 12 pp. text 1 p. references No figures	3/8/91 18 pp. Swendsen, 119 lines Bouzida, 50 lines Kumar, Absent	14 pp.	None	3/8/91 4 pp. On learning and Bouzida's draft
3 3/13/91 15 pp. total 12 pp. text 2 pp. appendix 1 p. references No figures	No review meeting	16 pp. [This draft contained a number of changes that had been requested but not made in the previous draft.]	3/18/91 4 pp. On changes made to text	None

4 4/24/91 14 pp. total 11 pp. text 1 p. appendix 2 pp. references No figures	No review meeting	30 pp. [This draft was produced by Swendsen, who was frustrated with Bouzida's inability to make requested changes.]	None	5/21/91 6 pp. On changes he made, and on readers and journals
5 5/3/91 21 pp. total 12 pp. text 1 p. appendix 2 pp. references 6 pp. figures	Two review meetings 5/3/91 6 pp. Swendsen, 54 lines Bouzida, 18 lines Kumar, 24 lines ———— 5/6/91 6 pp. Swendsen, 76 lines Bouzida, 26 lines Kumar, 1 line	13 pp.	5/3/91 2 pp. On changes Swendsen made and general progress on drafts	None
6 5/5/91 14 pp. total 11 pp. text 1 p. appendix 2 pp. references No figures	5/9/91 13 pages Swendsen, 149 lines Bouzida, 34 lines Kumar, 53 lines	16 pp.	5/13/91 4 pp. On changes	5/7/91 5 pp. On changes, learning, audience, theses, experience, and style
7 5/15/91 14 pp. total 11 pp. text 1 p. appendix 2 pp. references No figures	5/16/91 12 pages Swendsen, 166 lines Bouzida, 61 lines Kumar, Absent	14 pp.	None	None
8 5/17/91 14 pp. total 11 pp. text 1 p. appendix 2 pp. references No figures	5/17/91 13 pp. Swendsen, 153 lines Bouzida, 55 lines Kumar, 33 lines	15 pp.	None	None

9 5/20/91 20 pp. total 11 pp. text 1 p. appendix 2 pp. references 1 p. captions 5 pp. figures	No review meeting —drafts 9 through 14 were produced and passed back and forth quickly between Swendsen and Bouzida	11 pp.	5/20/91 None 4 pp. On changes in drafts 8 and 9	
10 5/21/91 20 pp. total 11 pp. text 1 p. appendix 2 pp. references 1 p. captions 5 pp. figures	No review meeting	6 pp. [There were few changes in this and the next several drafts. The physicists thought they were almost done and were preparing to have three scientists read the paper.]	None None	
11 5/23/91 20 pp. total 11 pp. text 1 p. appendix 2 pp. references 1 p. captions 5 pp. figures	No review meeting	5 pp.	None Interviewed on 6/3/91 (see draft 13).	
12 6/3/91 20 pp. total 11 pp. text 1 p. appendix 2 pp. references 1 p. captions 5 pp. figures	No review meeting —the meeting addressing drafts 12, 13, and 14 occurred on 6/4/91	4 pp. [They talked about being almost finished; however, this changed after they received feedback from the three scientists.]	None See next cell.	

13 6/3/91 20 pp. total 11 pp. text 1 p. appendix 2 pp. references 1 p. captions 5 pp. figures	No review meeting	6 pp.	None	6/3/91 5 pp. On changes in drafts and language
14 6/4/91 20 pp. total 11 pp. text 1 p. appendixes 2 pp. references 1 p. captions 5 pp. figures	6/4/91 12 pp. Swendsen, 131 lines Bouzida, 41 lines Kumar, 47 lines [This meeting was somewhat atypical —they addressed the concerns raised by their three readers.]	6 pp. [It is with this draft that they gradually began responding to the concerns of the three scientists who read the paper.]	None	6/5/91 2 pp. On the response of one of the readers and on journal placement
15 6/15/91 18 pp. total 11 pp text 1 p. appendix 2 pp. references 1 p. captions 3 pp. figures	No review meeting —this draft was addressed with the subsequent draft in the next review meeting	5 pp.	None	7/15/91; 7/30/91 5 pp.; 6 pp. On response of one reader and changes
16 6/16/91 16 pp. total 12 pp. text 1 p. appendix 2 pp. references 1 p. captions No figures	Two review meetings 6/16/91 14 pp. [for drafts 15 and 16] Swendsen, 140 lines Bouzida, 79 lines Kumar, 34 lines 8/6/91 11 pp. [follow-up on draft 16] Swendsen, 102 lines Bouzida, 60 lines Kumar, 38 lines	17 pp. [See concerns here with the comments made by their three readers.]	None	8/8/91 2 pp. On Bouzida's draft and on audience

17 8/9/91	8/9/91 17 pp.	18 pp.	8/12/91 None
21 pp. total 12 pp. text 1 p. appendix 3 pp. references 1 p. captions 4 pp. figures	Swendsen, 165 lines Bouzida, 123 lines Kumar, 29 lines [Bouzida's contributions focused on the physics.]	[Still working out responses to their readers.]	5 pp. On changes in last several drafts
18 8/16/91	No review meeting —the meeting addressing this and the following two drafts occurred the day draft 20 was produced	8 pp.	None None
25 pp. total 12 pp. text 1 p. appendix 3 pp. references 1 p. caption 8 pp. figures		[Almost finished —begin final changes.]	
19 8/19/91	No review meeting —discussed with drafts 18 and 20	7 pp.	None None
25 pp. total 13 pp. text 1 p. appendix 2 pp. references 1 p. captions 8 pp. figures			
20 8/21/91	8/21/91 14 pp.	13 pp.	None None
26 pp. total 13 pp. text 1 p. appendix 3 pp. references 1 p. captions 8 pp. figures	Swendsen, 176 lines Bouzida, 55 lines Kumar, 30 lines [Meeting for this and the two previous drafts.]	[Still addressing reader concerns.]	
21 8/23/91	8/23/91 10 pp.	11 pp.	None None
26 pp. total 13 pp. text 1 p. appendix 2 pp. references 2 pp. captions 8 pp. figures	Swendsen, 118 lines Bouzida, 55 lines Kumar, 17 lines [Final draft meeting —made final changes.]	[In this draft they were still reworking and fine-tuning their problem statement.]	

22 8/23/91	No review meeting	6 pp.	8/23/91	10/2/91
26 pp. total	—corrected surface-level problems	[Final draft submitted to *Physical Review D.*]	2 pp.	5 pp.
13 pp. text			On com- pletion of draft	On com- pletion of draft
1 p. appendix				
3 pp. references			[I also interviewed Swendsen on 1/7/92 and 2/10/92.]	
1 pp. captions				
8 pp. figures				

Note. This table summarizes the data I collected during the production of the DOMC paper, which was the focus of my analyses. In it, I document general information about each of the drafts, the exchanges in the review meetings, the draft analyses, and the interviews I conducted to obtain additional information about the drafts and about the interactions and activities that surrounded them.

From A. M. Blakeslee, *Journal of Business and Technical Communication (11)* 2, 125–169. Copyright © 1997 by A. M. Blakeslee. Reprinted by permission of Sage Publications, Inc.

[a]For figures, one page corresponds to one figure.

[b]One line = one line of text.

NOTES

1. Carnegie Mellon University is a private research university in Pittsburgh, PA, with an approximate enrollment of 6500 students, one-third of whom are graduate students.

2. Just over one-half of the approximately 60 to 65 graduate students in physics at Carnegie Mellon at this time were from countries other than the United States. Many American programs have large, nonnative student populations because foreign students are well trained, and because some prefer attending graduate school in the United States due to the strength of its programs and institutions. In some programs and research groups, lack of fluency in English poses problems both in day-to-day communications and in publishing. This was not the case in the group I studied.

3. To facilitate the comparison of changes and the cross-referencing of relevant commentary, I used a program called Prep Editor (Chandhok et al., 1992, 1996). This program allowed me to construct and link five columns in which I placed, side by side, changes and rhetorical moves in the text, along with related comments from the meetings and from my interviews with the participants. The five columns I created included:

    1. "Text," in which I placed the content of each paragraph in each section of the draft.

    2. "Changes made (text)," in which I documented all changes Bouzida made in the current draft (for comparison I recorded the revisions and the previous versions of the text).

3. "Comments (changes made)," in which I placed all comments the physicists wrote on the previous draft and stated in their discussions, as well as notes from interviews that related to the changes made in the text (I clearly labeled the source of each comment).

4. "Suggested changes (text)," in which I placed all comments that Swendsen wrote in the current version of the text during the review meetings.

5. "Comments (suggested changes)," in which I placed all comments concerning the changes that the physicists made in the meetings or during my interviews (I clearly labeled the source of each comment).

I completed these analyses for each draft of the paper and had a total of 256 pages of horizontally printed five-column analyses.

4. Gieryn (1978) also addressed how the first paper that is written in a new problem area will likely require more preparation time on the parts of its authors than subsequent papers (p. 105).

5. To validate my interpretations of my data I relied primarily on the responses of my informants—both those I interviewed outside of the group and the participants. I did not use independent, outside coders as I do not believe that reliability is a viable tool in situated work or that it can ever be attained, particularly given the requirements of such work for immersion in the context being studied. As an alternative to traditional approaches to validity, I adopted Mishler's (1990) inductive and grounded approach to validation, which "involves a continual dialectic between data, analysis, and theory" (p. 428). Mishler advocated looking to standards that are relevant and meaningful for interpretive research and that are within our grasp.

6. This prominent positioning of published scientific texts in rhetorical scholarship, especially famous texts, has a long and also productive history. Early works in the field successfully challenged the epistemological privilege of science and its ontological claims to truth by analyzing and revealing the rhetorical features of scientific prose style (see, e.g., Burke, 1967; Campbell, 1975, 1989; Crinsmore & Farnsworth, 1989; Daniel, 1982; Halloran, 1978; Halloran & Whitburn, 1982; Lipson, 1985; Moran, 1984; Paradis, 1983; Stephens, 1975, 1983; Zappen, 1975, 1979). These works revealed the contingency and subjectivity inherent in the scientific enterprise. More recent works, like those by Bazerman (1988), Gross (1990), Myers (1990), Prelli (1989), and Winsor (1996), built on and expanded this previous scholarship by considering contextual and other rhetorical issues in addition to stylistic and linguistic ones (additional examples of this recent work include Bazerman, 1981, 1984a, 1984b, 1985; Blakeslee, 1992, 1993, 1994, 1997; Fahnestock, 1986; Fahnestock & Secor, 1988; Gragson & Selzer, 1990; Gross, 1988; Haas, 1994; Halloran, 1984; Journet, 1990; Kaufer & Carley, 1993; Miller, 1992; Myers, 1985, 1991, 1996; Paul & Charney,

1995; Reeves, 1990; Rymer, 1988; Selzer, 1993; Sullivan, 1996; Thacker & Stratman, 1995; Zappen, 1985, 1987, 1989, 1991).

7. Prelli (1989) addressed interactions with audiences in his work, but mostly in terms of imaginary dialogues; he said rhetors should select ideas and arguments while engaging in at least an imaginary dialogue with the audience (p. 68).

2

Planning to Persuade: Strategies for Publicizing Ideas and Addressing Audiences

From the first choices scientists make about their research, they are rhetorically positioning their work. In this and the next several chapters, I extend investigations of how scientists position new research to consider how Swendsen, Bouzida, and Kumar deliberately planned and carried out various strategies to influence and persuade their constituents, both those within their own community of physics and those in biology and chemistry.[1] I focus in this chapter on how the physicists selected and defined their research problem, and on how their audiences' differing conceptions of this problem influenced both the physicists' definition and their subsequent research. I also show how the physicists disseminated their preliminary findings at a physics conference to position and gain support for their work prior to publishing it. (I save discussion of how the physicists prepared and positioned the main DOMC paper for later chapters.) My findings in this chapter show how Swendsen, Bouzida, and Kumar, rather than relying on a single rhetorical event to persuade their audiences (e.g., publication), deliberately engaged in ongoing rhetorical activity from the initial stages of their work.

FORMULATING A RESEARCH PROBLEM: AN INITIAL RHETORICAL MOVE

Arguably, then, the physicists began targeting and trying to persuade their audiences, not when they started thinking about or writing the DOMC paper, but when they initially formulated their research problem. According to Gieryn (1978), selecting a research problem is one of the most consequential decisions that scientists make (p. 96).[2] Swendsen also addressed the importance of this task for scientists. He said, "There's a basic problem in all of science of how you choose problems. How you decide what's important. This is highlighted when you present it…. That's a crucial factor in one's career, finding out what's doable and what's important and of value" (Swendsen, personal communication, March 8, 1991). Implicit in Swendsen's comment is a concern with the audiences that will eventually judge the problem's value. Prelli (1989) addressed this rhetorical dimension of problem formulation when he said that scientists choose the issues they address and then persuade their peers that those issues are significant (p. 144). According to Prelli, both the choice of a problem in science, and the choices of how and where to insert the claims addressing it, are rhetorical ones (p. 144).[3] Audience is thus a central concern in scientific problem formulation.

For the physicists, the problem that led to the DOMC work centered around the question, "What is the most efficient and reliable method for simulating biological molecules?" Or as Bouzida said, "We're interested in simulation methods and the efficiencies in those methods" (personal communication, January 18, 1991). Swendsen characterized this problem, saying, "Our concern is with the problem of simulating organic molecules. We're interested in properties of biologically interesting molecules, and we're interested in them from the point of view of computer simulation…. So, getting better ways of simulating current molecular dynamics" (personal communication, January 16, 1991). Swendsen, Bouzida, and Kumar felt that the current approaches to performing such simulations could be improved. They also believed that the Dynamically Optimized Monte Carlo method, which they preferred, was superior to the molecular dynamics method biologists and chemists preferred.

According to one of the scientists I interviewed, molecular dynamics is a straightforward method that does not require many decisions (David, personal communication, June 7, 1991). David said this is why biologists and chemists preferred it: "MD … is more attractive because the real dynamics of the system are put in; it deals with Newton's equations. So in a sense it's the most straightforward approach. You do calculations in real time" (personal communication, June 7, 1991). However, he also addressed some of the limitations of MD: "The problem is you can't go very far in real time—a few picoseconds … , which is something we've been concerned with. Most simulations don't get to the point you want them to with such short times. So the idea of bypassing the act and using a method that allows you to get to equilibrium state quicker is attractive" (personal communication, June 7, 1991). The method David alluded to in this statement is Monte Carlo, which he characterized as a creative and more flexible method that entails more decisions. David's latter statement also captured the physicists' primary concern in carrying out their research—finding a more efficient method to simulate biological molecules.

The DOMC method the physicists ended up using in their research was a modification of the Monte Carlo method that biologists and chemists had found to be less preferable. (Northrup and McCammon had claimed that MC required more computer time than MD, a claim the physicists later disputed.) The physicists said that they chose DOMC primarily because of its flexibility and randomness. Addressing what he perceived to be the advantages of this method, Swendsen said,

> You can play a lot of games with it—varying moves.... We have optimization methods that account for the inhomogeneity of proteins.... Have a small number of molecules, so can do things efficiently. [You can] simulate properties of the molecules faster than standard molecules. [You] can also yield them down and get the right configuration.... We're trying to apply these methods to a protein, glucagon. There's a lot that's known about its structure. We can do the simulations more efficiently than molecular dynamics, and we're making progress on the annealing problem. (personal communication, January 16, 1991)

The physicists believed that DOMC was both more efficient and more flexible than MD, despite Northrup and McCammon's claims, and therefore more desirable for performing these simulations.

In addition to expressing their preference for the DOMC method, the physicists also expressed concerns with the ways in which biologists and chemists approached the simulations, more generally. One of these concerns had to do with the size of the molecules these scientists simulated. Swendsen, as mentioned in chapter 1, believed in simulating smaller molecules first and then moving on to the larger ones: "The approach of experts is to take the smallest molecule you can then go to bigger ones and see what changes.... [You] don't start with big ones [since] you get hung up on computer time" (Swendsen, personal communication, July 15, 1991). According to the physicists, chemists' and biologists' preference for larger molecules was problematic:

> You can't just start off applying something to a big problem. Problems change and new elements come in. You have to start out small and simple. That's the way it's done in the physics community. I think part of it is the community— they're just not used to doing something this way.... There's a tendency among those who do simulations to go right after the big stuff, not mess around with the small stuff. They get messed up pretty fast and have to go back. (Swendsen, personal communication, July 15, 1991)

The distinction between larger and smaller molecules, in the physicists' view, had significant implications for this kind of work.

Another concern the physicists expressed with the biologists' and chemists' approaches to the simulations related to their uses of canned, or prepackaged, programs. Bouzida said, "There are groups that buy simulation packages and use them as black boxes" (personal communication, January 18, 1991). According to Kumar, such canned programs can lead scientists to draw premature and unsubstantiated conclusions: "There are problems with the groups using the packaged programs as black boxes. They more easily jump to conclusions and there's not as strong of a scientific basis" (personal communication, January 18, 1991). Swendsen said that such programs "are very user friendly and very easy to manipulate. Very easy to get results with," and, consequently, chemists and biologists prefer them (personal communication, November 27, 1996). The physicists, on the other hand, preferred using original programs tailored to the particular simulation problems. Swendsen said, "to implement what we've been doing then they have to write their own programs," which, he added, requires a substantial amount of work (personal communication, November 27, 1996). He also said that "you have to have a really strong reason for doing that" (personal communication, November 27, 1996). For Kumar the reason seemed apparent: "Our work is sort of like making better bearings to make the wheel run more smoothly … furthering the technology to make it better" (personal communication, January 18, 1991).

In summary, the members of these various communities approached the simulations of these molecules very differently. Although biologists and chemists preferred using MD, and although they preferred to simulate large systems and use prepackaged or "canned" simulation programs to do so, the physicists preferred using the more flexible DOMC method and using it first with smaller molecules. These differences in how biologists and chemists approached and carried out the simulations posed a number of challenges for the physicists as they began to present their work and as they endeavored to influence these scientists' perspectives. In fact, the differences in approaches and viewpoints prompted the physicists to act very deliberately as they began to position the DOMC work. In the next section I examine one of their actions, showing how they presented an early version of the work to members of their own community in the hope of obtaining longer term support for it in biology and chemistry.

PRESENTING EARLY RESULTS:
BEGINNING THE PROCESS OF ADDRESSING FAMILIAR
AND UNFAMILIAR AUDIENCES

Because of the variations in what the different communities believed about MD and DOMC, and how they approached the simulations, the physicists started, very early, to plan ways to address and influence their audiences.

They focused their efforts, primarily, on ways to convince biologists and chemists of the value of their methods. Getting published was not the problem—persuasion was, as Swendsen commented:

> We knew we could get the paper published. The whole thing was how we could best get the ideas across, which, of course, that brings up another thing we were talking about—that the goal was not to get the paper published. The goal was to get the ideas accepted in the community that we were addressing.... I was really very interested in changing practice and changing the way people attack these problems in their areas. (personal communication, November, 27, 1996)

The physicists believed that publication alone would not guarantee that the scientists in these other communities would accept their work. As a result, they decided to publicize and publicly position the work using a variety of strategies. For example, the physicists presented preliminary findings from the work at a conference in their own discipline, gave talks at colloquia within their own and at a neighboring institution, and gave a draft of the DOMC paper to three scientists for feedback. I address two of these strategies in subsequent chapters—giving talks at colloquia and giving a draft of the paper to other scientists (chaps. 3, 4, and 5). Here I address the physicists' early presentation of their findings at a physics conference and how they used this strategy to obtain support for the work, both within their own and in the other communities they were addressing.

The physicists began the conference paper approximately 1 year after they had begun the DOMC project, and 1 year before they started writing papers about it for publication. Swendsen presented the paper at the annual conference of the Statistical Physics Society. The physicists also published the paper in a proceedings from the conference (Bouzida, Kumar, & Swendsen, 1991). The audience at this conference was comprised of other physicists who were also interested in statistical mechanics. When he described this audience to me in an interview, Swendsen said, "There was nothing controversial in this group.... This audience was strongly biased toward Monte Carlo, so it was friendly in that sense. Also, they were people I knew, so there wasn't a lot at stake here" (personal communication, March 1, 1991). He also said that the audience would generally be interested in and receptive to the DOMC work:

> This was the first external presentation of this work. This group is interested in any kinds of improvements in methods and simulations, so anything here is of interest. They're also interested in new applications and new fields.... So different ones in the group would be interested in this. (personal communication, March 1, 1991)

Swendsen made a very deliberate decision to present the DOMC work first to this supportive audience. He knew this community, agreed with it, and had a secure and respected place in it.

Brandt (1990) pointed out in her work that written texts are not unproblematic end products, that the lives of texts do not end once they have been published. Instead, texts are "documents that are themselves gaining problematic public life in social arenas" (p. 11). The text, she said, "is the territory on which détente must begin" (p. 11). My work with the physicists shows this détente occurring long before publication. When Swendsen discussed the conference paper, he expressed two concerns: letting other scientists know about the work, and establishing its interest and value. Swendsen said that the physicists wanted to inform these scientists that they were "making progress in an interesting field, and ... developing new Markovian methods that are powerful and can be used in other applications" (personal communication, March 1, 1991). The physicists' work, according to Swendsen, was not at a stage yet where it was ready to be acted on or used, but it was far enough along, he believed, to at least be presented to and considered by their familiar audiences. He said, "These are methods they could use, but we didn't stress that. We didn't want them to jump in before it was published. We said it was applicable in other cases, but we didn't say which ones" (personal communication, March 1, 1999).

The physicists' objective for this paper was to obtain support for their work that would hopefully carry over to its presentation to biologists and chemists. They were especially concerned with reaching the scientists who could end up reviewing the work:

> When you're publishing, you don't want someone going to the referee and their not knowing anything. We're anticipating refereeing problems. We'll have no problems with journals inside physics—they know me and have the same background.... Eventually we'll get it through. We can argue these things. It's easier, though, if the ref has heard of them already. If they know them and that it's something good and something interesting is going on they'll be less likely to dismiss it. (Swendsen, personal communication, March 1, 1991)

To build the case for their argument, they were really just addressing a segment of their ultimate audience with the intent of eventually reaching a much larger segment.[4]

This approach of presenting work first to a congenial audience also reflects a persuasive strategy discussed by Perelman and Olbrechts-Tyteca (1969). These scholars addressed the sort of positioning strategy where, "Unless circumstances determine the audience, an argument can be presented first to one group of people, and then to another, and gain by the adherence of the first, or, more oddly, by their rejection of it" (p. 109). Knorr (1979) addressed a similar strategy: "In the case of impending criticism, a special presentation of the results might be arranged for an internal audience, or 'severe critics' found for an internal review of the paper, in order to better identify the expectable counterarguments" (p. 356). In discussing their audiences for the DOMC work, Swendsen once said, "The work is highly controversial in chemistry though, which comes later" (personal communication, March 1, 1991). Through their gradual positioning of the work, the physicists hoped to get scientists used to their ideas before the scientists were asked to critique them.

Swendsen's reflections on how they composed the conference paper, and what they included in it, further illustrate how the physicists differentiated their audiences and how they adapted their rhetorical strategies for these audiences. When he talked about the paper, Swendsen addressed three important issues: what the physicists felt they could take for granted in the paper, what they felt they needed to present in it, and how they felt they should present the information to address their audiences' concerns. He contrasted the approach they took for this familiar physics audience with the approach that they were taking in the DOMC paper, which was addressed to all of their audiences. He said:

> The talk was much different from our paper. There were a lot of pictures, few words, little by way of equations. This would have been much different for a biological audience. Here we did not have to explain what any of the methods were; for example, molecular dynamics, Monte Carlo, standard optimization. We would have to explain that to anyone outside of the field, but this audience knew it. (personal communication, March 1, 1991)

The physicists seemed to be very aware of the differences in the knowledge and concerns of their audiences, even though, at this early stage, this awareness was based mostly on a general sense of these communities—the physicists had not yet interacted directly with the biologists or chemists. As another example of this awareness, Swendsen addressed what his audience for this presentation would likely know, versus what they would not know and need to have explained:

> No one knows anything about biological systems or materials. They know the method codes. MD, for example, they would know ... immediately, but they would not know biological systems.... Biologists and chemists were interested in different questions and validity checks. The group this was presented to didn't have those concerns. (personal communication, March 1, 1991)

As an insider in this community, Swendsen knew the scientists he was addressing, and he knew, from his previous interactions with them, what their concerns and interests were (Russell, 1997, pp. 538, 541). He could predict, with a reasonable amount of certainty, what they would know and want, or need to know. Swendsen's remarks also echo Perelman and Olbrechts-Tyteca's (1969) comments about how "the nature of the audience … will determine to a great extent both the direction the arguments will take and the character, the significance that will be attributed to them" (p. 30).

The rhetorical character of the physicists' presentation was perhaps most evident in the text itself. The physicists started the conference paper by stating very clearly that this was a preliminary report of work that was still in progress.[5] Their first sentence read, "The methods described in this paper concern some work we have been doing recently on the simulation of large molecules: proteins, nucleic acids, etc." (Bouzida et al., 1991, p. 193, paragraph 1, sentence 1). A bit later in the text they articulated the purpose and scope of the paper: "The full story of what progress we have made in this search is too long to discuss in a brief talk. However, we would like to discuss our basic approach leaving some important features of how to deal effectively with the long-wavelength modes for another time" (Bouzida et al., 1991, p. 194, paragraph 4). The physicists said that they were less concerned with making an argument in this paper than with conveying useful information:

> We were not at all concerned in this situation with making and substantiating an argument per se. That would come later.… We had done a thorough job of testing, so we gave an indication of the things we had gone through. We also had to explain why the questions were different. The questions in biology are entirely different; very different set of questions. (personal communication, March 1, 1991)

Swendsen attributed this informative stance to the nature of the audience: "This group is interested in any kinds of improvements in methods and simulations, so anything here is of interest. They're also interested in new applications and new fields.… So, different ones in the group would be interested in this" (personal communication, March 1, 1999).

Despite their claims that argumentation was secondary in the conference paper, the physicists still made numerous persuasive statements. Even their abstract made a fairly strong claim for their approach:

> By relaxing the usual restriction of algorithms to Markov processes, *we are able to perform optimized simulations* [emphasis added] that take into account the inhomogeneity and anisotropy inherent in these systems. *Our approach samples configurational space more efficiently than either standard Monte Carlo or molecular dynamics methods* [emphasis added]. (Bouzida et al., 1991, p. 193, abstract)

In other parts of their text they also made statements about the value and efficiency of the DOMC approach and the importance and significance of their findings. For example, the paragraph addressing the speed and efficiency of their simulation results read:

> We have lifted the restriction to Markov processes by making use of the information gathered during the simulation to optimize the local Monte Carlo moves [4]. *We were then able to show* [emphasis added] by explicit simulations of models with exact solutions, that if reasonable limits are not exceeded, *the resulting algorithms substantially increase the speed of the simulation without introducing any measurable deviation from the correct equilibrium behavior* [emphasis added]. (Bouzida et al., 1991, p. 194, paragraph 7)

And in the paragraph addressing the benefits of DOMC, they said:

> Although this method, which we denote as Dynamically Optimized Monte Carlo (DOMC) is based on an analysis of a simple harmonic oscillator, *these equations turn out to be remarkably robust* [emphasis added] when applied to a wide variety of Hamiltonians. (Bouzida et al., 1991, p. 194, paragraph 8, last sentence)

The physicists did much more in the paper than simply inform their audience about their work.

Another interesting feature of the physicists' conference paper is how they positioned themselves in relation to their audiences. In this initial presentation of their work, the physicists distinguished themselves from the communities they identified as being concerned with the simulations. In their first paragraph of the text, they said, "These simulations are becoming increasingly important in chemistry, biology, and medicine [1, 2]" (Bouzida et al., 1991, p. 193, paragraph 1, sentence 2). In contrast, the corresponding part of the DOMC text included physics in this list: "In recent years, much effort and computational resources have been devoted to simulating macromolecules. These molecules, which include polymers, proteins, and nucleic acids, are of great importance in physics, chemistry, biology, and medicine [1, 2]" (Bouzida, Kumar, & Swendsen, draft 21 of the DOMC paper, August 23, 1991, paragraph 1, sentences 1 and 2).

In the next part of the conference paper, the physicists continued their outsider perspective. The second paragraph read:

> There are many questions that biologists and chemists ask about the properties of large molecules. Some of these questions concern the short-time development of the molecule.... However, most of the questions concern equilibrium properties. The equilibrium configuration is of prime importance in determining biological function. (Bouzida et al., 1991, p. 193, paragraph 2)

They presented a similar formulation in the DOMC paper, but they removed the statement that attributed the questions to biologists and chemists:

In developing new methods, we must keep in mind the nature of the system and the types of questions that are asked. Some of these questions concern the dynamics of short-time behavior ..., and the only current option is MD. However, most questions concern equilibrium properties. The equilibrium configuration is of major importance in determining biological function, and free-energy calculations are needed to predict and understand biochemical reactions. (Bouzida, Kumar, & Swendsen, draft 21 of the DOMC paper, August 23, 1991, paragraph 10)

The physicists' formulations in the DOMC paper, in general, tended to be more inclusive. The DOMC paper contained far fewer statements than the conference paper that portrayed biologists and chemists as others (see chap. 5 for a significant exception to this). It also contained more statements portraying these scientists as part of a larger interdisciplinary community to which the physicists also belonged.

The physicists viewed this presentation to their peers in physics as an important initial strategy for positioning and promoting the DOMC work. They also viewed it as just one part of what would be an ongoing and deliberate process by which they would establish contact with and gain the adherence of all of their audiences. This process seems to resemble the one that Law and Williams (1982) described when they addressed how scientists develop a usable and appealing product:

They assess the likely value of their product to this group or that. They design the product in such a way that its value will be as clear as possible to potential users. They *package* and *place* it with the same considerations in mind. They act, then, in many ways like entrepreneurs who combine resources to generate a product that will ensure an optimum return. (p. 537)

The physicists carefully planned their entry into and participation in the communities they were targeting. They recognized that different formulations and presentations of the work would function together, and not discretely, in their overall persuasive efforts. However, the process in which they engaged, although well planned, was also sometimes problematic, filled with uncertainty and challenges, especially as they began addressing their audiences in biology and chemistry.[6]

NOTES

1. For examples of previous examinations of how scientists position new research, see Callon, Law, and Rip (1986a), Latour (1987), Latour & Woolgar (1986), Law & Williams (1982), and Swales (1990).

2. Gieryn (1978) also addressed the risks involved in moving into new areas, which is what the physicists were trying to do. These risks, he said, result from scien-

tists' lack of associations, knowledge of the area, and possibly even skills (p. 105). The two former issues became significant for the physicists when they interacted with a biophysicist and chemist as they were composing the DOMC paper (see chaps. 4 and 5).

3. In the fields of sociology and rhetoric, numerous other scholars have also addressed the importance of problem selection in scientific work. Knorr (1979), for example, talked about how scientists begin with an "asset," or a perceived solution, which raises the question around which the scientists later organize the paper (p. 362). Zuckerman (1978), addressed how scientists sometimes find it more difficult to locate research problems than answers (p. 73), and she identified two criteria for selecting and evaluating scientific problems: their assessed importance and the feasibility of finding a solution (p. 82). Social processes within science, she said, also play a role (p. 82), as they certainly did for the physicists. Zuckerman (1978, p. 86), along with Gieryn, also addressed factors that encourage continuity in a problem area. Gieryn (1978) addressing these factors, said:

> Accumulation of research experience in a problem area may mean that less preparatory time is required to produce each additional paper on these problems. The first paper worked out in a problem area will probably require more preparation time than the tenth. Retention of long-standing interests in a problem area may make it easier for a scientist to satisfy motivations and social expectations to make contributions to the scientific literature. (p. 105)

These comments offer one explanation for some of the difficulties the physicists encountered composing the DOMC paper, especially with respect to why it may have taken them as many drafts as it did to complete it.

4. The physicists' strategy in this case also seems consistent with Law's (1986) characterization of the construction and use of actor-networks in science. The aim here, Law said, is to endow the key point with the capacity to act far beyond its place of origin (p. 68). Callon, Law, & Rip (1986b) similarly addressed how scientists try to build up a structured world in texts that allows them to act on others at a distance (p. 10). Russell (1997) talked about how scholars try to marshal longer networks (p. 524). Through texts, these scholars contended, authors both construct a world and persuade others (Callon et al., 1986b, p. 11).

5. Swales (1990) also characterized such presentations as reports of work in progress, which, in many respects, was what the physicists had written (p. 178). Swales also noted how presentations are often versions of research articles that have not yet been published (p. 178), which was also the case in this situation. In fact, the physicists used the written conference paper as a basis for their initial draft of the DOMC paper (see chap. 6.). Numerous similarities, as well as some noteworthy differences, existed between the two texts. An examination of parts of both texts reveals some of these similarities and differences and points to their significance in relation to the different audiences the physicists were targeting.

6. Lave and Wenger (1991), in the context of their discussion of communities of practice, addressed how the work and understanding of newcomers bear complex and changing relations with ongoing work processes (p. 89). All of this, they said, has implications for the deepening and changing understanding for all members of the community (p. 89).

3

Getting to Know Familiar and Unfamiliar Audiences: Learning About Audiences Within One's Own and Across Different Communities

In the previous chapter, I considered the strategies the physicists used to begin publicly positioning their DOMC work. In this chapter, I examine how they learned about and became familiar with all of their audiences for the work.[1] Generally, I address how Bouzida, a newcomer both to physics as well as to these other domains, and Swendsen, an experienced practitioner in physics but a newcomer to biology and chemistry, learned about these audiences. I was especially interested in my research in examining how experts, like Swendsen, adapt to new audiences and communities of practice, especially interdisciplinary ones that may not have recognizable or well-defined structures, or established histories with respect to interacting and communicating. I found in my work that knowing how to adapt one's writing to a particular community entails more than having a body of knowledge that is simply learned at some point in time and always retained. Rather, it is a tool or a skill that requires continual updating as communities shift and change and as individuals enter and leave them. In particular, I show descriptively with my data how audience analysis is a social enterprise that entails direct interactions with actual audience members. Interaction in such a view is key to knowing and reaching an audience.

My observations of how the physicists got to know and interact with their audiences, both in their own discipline of physics and in biology and chemistry, suggest a model for audience analysis based on social interaction. In this model, authors interact directly with actual audience members to understand how their audiences might respond to their ideas, including what attitudes they might bring to them, and how, therefore, they should present their ideas given such attitudes and potential responses. The model of audience analysis I present here, then, consists of two primary operations, both of which depend on social inputs: (a) getting to know and understand one's interlocutors, and (b) determining how to reach and influence them. Because of the primacy of interactions in both of these operations, this model also supports a dynamic conception of audience analysis: Ongoing interactions allow authors to monitor and keep track of the changing concerns of audiences.

However, my findings also suggest that this social interaction model may need to be qualified at times. In particular, Swendsen, Bouzida, and Kumar occasionally made trade-offs because of time and other constraints they faced (e.g., they chose efficiency over time-consuming immersion in the other communities), and they sometimes faced consequences as a result of these trade-offs. For example, on some level the three physicists chose not to immerse themselves in these communities to the extent that seemed to be needed to make the biologists and chemists receptive to their ideas. I show, therefore, that the concerns the physicists expressed for their audience were not always the same as doing what it would take to bridge the gap successfully between themselves and their unfamiliar interlocutors.

A final important point that I make in this chapter is that the physicists' efforts to get to know their audiences extended beyond the publication of their work. They did not give up trying to learn about and get to know the biologists and chemists, even after they abandoned them as the immediate audience for the DOMC paper. This is evidenced by, among other things, Bouzida's and Kumar's postdoctoral commitments within these other communities. The ongoing quality of such activity also highlights that initiation into a community may take years, which raises the important question of whether there are ways to speed up such processes or whether they simply require this slow cumulative experience.

LEARNING ABOUT AUDIENCES IN ONE'S OWN FIELD:
THE ROLES OF INTERACTION AND EXPOSURE
TO A COMMUNITY'S DISCOURSE

One way we can begin to understand the process of getting to know audiences is by following Bouzida as he was initiated into his own field. This initiation, which occurred gradually, entailed interacting with other physicists and being exposed to the community's discourse, a process that seems typical for graduate students in his field. For example, one of the physicists I interviewed for my research said:

Audience knowledge comes from attending meetings. Actually, it starts in graduate school I think. Your advisor uses the buzzwords, and if you're clever you ask what they mean. You also read papers and ask about what you don't understand. You also go to meetings, which are steeped in the appropriate jargon, and if you hear it often enough you start to believe you understand it. (Rich, personal communication, August 9, 1991)

Porter (1992) argued that individuals who wish to be authors must undergo such socialization in order to attain identification and membership in a community (p. 112).[2] A writer's job in writing, Porter said, entails understanding the community and adopting an appropriate ethos within it (p. 112). This applies to newcomers as well as experts. For graduate students in physics, attaining such understanding seems to require reading, listening, and questioning.

Swendsen also said that learning about one's community, and acquiring the skill to effectively address it, requires time, accumulated experience, and interaction. Further, such learning extends beyond the limited period of graduate studies. Swendsen noted, in addition, that learning about one's community, and what its members believe and find acceptable, makes it easier to construct arguments:

Knowing your readers affects what you say and write. It takes a lot of time to get to know them—*10 years say* [emphasis added]—and then judging them becomes easier. There are acceptance of certain types of general arguments, which you have to learn. When you know them you know when all you have to do is wave your hand versus driving something very hard. (personal communication, May 7, 1991)

According to Swendsen, getting to know one's audience requires engaging actively in a field by giving talks, meeting people at conferences, talking to people on the telephone, and exchanging e-mail (personal communication, May 7, 1991). Without such engagement, he said, authors—especially new authors—experience difficulties with their audiences. Describing these difficulties as they pertained to Bouzida, he once said, "The audience is a tough problem for him [Bouzida] or for any grad student. They haven't met the audience yet. In some sense, I haven't either [referring to the biologists and chemists the three physicists were addressing]" (personal communication, May 7, 1991).[3] Another physicist I interviewed also addressed the difficulties that physics graduate students often have with their audiences. He said, "One of the biggest problems a graduate student has is understanding how their work fits in with what's out there—a sense of its relative importance; also, confidence that their work makes a valid contribution. It's not going to set the world on fire, but it will fill a hole" (Brad, personal communication, August 21, 1991).[4]

Bouzida's experiences giving two talks on the DOMC work illustrate these difficulties. Bouzida presented the first talk at a colloquium sponsored by the Chemistry Department at Carnegie Mellon. His audience included professors, postdoctoral fellows, and other graduate students, primarily from chemistry. (This talk fulfilled a requirement of Bouzida's department stipulating that students present their work orally to a group of their peers and professors before completing their theses.) Bouzida presented the second talk at a lunchtime colloquium sponsored by his own department. When he described his audiences for these talks, Bouzida expressed confidence that he understood their concerns. However, his experiences with the two talks suggest that his confidence may have been premature.

In the first talk, his presentation to the chemists, Bouzida spent most of his time defining and explaining the DOMC method. He addressed the problems that he and Swendsen and Kumar had with Northrup and McCammon's work, and he argued that Monte Carlo was more efficient than molecular dynamics for performing simulations. He said he took this approach in the talk because of the chemists' unfamiliarity with the DOMC method and because of their long-standing preference for MD.

The chemists, however, were not convinced by Bouzida's arguments. In their comments and questions after his talk, they expressed their continued skepticism regarding MC, and they sought additional proof of the efficiency of the method. Their questions, and the difficulty Bouzida seemed to have responding to them (he relied extensively on Swendsen for assistance), suggest that Bouzida had not yet anticipated many of his audience members' concerns. His understanding of the chemists and of what they would be looking for and expecting from this work seemed superficial. He had begun to think through what information they would likely want, but he had not thought through how to present that information in a persuasive or compelling manner.

Bouzida's second talk posed similar challenges. In this talk, Bouzida again focused the content of the paper on what he believed to be the concerns these scientists had. Specifically, he believed the physicists understood and were more receptive toward Monte Carlo and therefore did not need to be informed about or convinced of its merits. Thus, instead of defending Monte Carlo or comparing Monte Carlo and molecular dynamics, he focused the talk on a different topic, simulated annealing. He also seemed to be much less formal and more relaxed with this talk; he appeared to be just discussing rather than formally presenting the work.

The responses and interactions that occurred at the physics talk were much different, and, to at least my surprise, even more antagonistic than those that occurred with the chemists. The physicists began asking questions while the talk was still in progress (rather than waiting until the end as is customarily done), and the tone of many of these questions seemed confrontational—members of the audience questioned the physicists' ideas, approaches, and assumptions. This questioning may have resulted from Bouzida sharing with his physicist colleagues a vocabulary for arguing, or it may have also resulted from the faculty at the talk viewing it as their responsibility to introduce Bouzida to the kind of argumentation and response he would likely encounter as a full-fledged member of the profession. Thus, their hostility may have actually been signaling acceptance and initiation into the community.[5]

Because Swendsen and Kumar were not able to attend the physics talk, Bouzida was left on his own to respond to his colleagues' objections. In Swendsen's absence, one member of Bouzida's thesis committee, who was familiar with the group's work, helped Bouzida out by rephrasing and responding to some of the questions. The feedback Bouzida received from this talk was unexpected and surprising, as well as informative. It was surprising in that the physics audience seemed more skeptical of the DOMC work than the chemistry audience, and it was informative in that this feedback suggested concerns and objections that the physicists needed to address better—objections that Bouzida had not anticipated.

Bouzida had differentiated his audiences for the two talks on the basis of his perceptions of them (he took a vessel approach, showing a concern, primarily, with filling them with knowledge). However, he had not anticipated the concerns that both groups might express in response to his presentations. In other words, Bouzida did not attend to the persuasive and argumentative appeals, and other presentation issues, in addition to content, that need to be considered by authors when they seek to persuade different audiences. One could conclude from these situations that Bouzida had not yet acquired the knowledge of his audience that lets an author know "when all you have to do is wave your hand versus driving something very hard" (Swendsen, personal communication, May 7, 1991). Bouzida's experiences delivering these presentations, and the responses he received to them, were, in many respects, just a beginning. The socialization process he was undergoing was ongoing and gradual (see chap. 6 for additional discussion of this process and of how it occurred as Bouzida composed the early drafts of the DOMC paper).

In fact, my findings also suggest that such socialization—in particular, interaction and exposure to a community's discourse—remains important even for experienced members of a domain. Rather than becoming complacent about their audiences, experienced practitioners must continually revise and update their knowledge structures of these audiences. Audiences are dynamic entities that shift and change as scientists move in and out of shared project spaces. David Lazarus, past editor in chief of *Physical Review* and *Physical Review Letters*, pointed out:

> Most of us are strong interactors. First, you read their papers and you may correspond with the authors before meeting them. Second, you go to conferences and meet people.... So it's sort of a natural kind of thing that arises in the profession. Interaction—communicating and going to meetings. (personal communication, September 19, 1991)

According to Swendsen, and other physicists I interviewed, the understanding that is built up through such interactions facilitates addressing one's audience. Swendsen, for example, said that personally knowing specific members of one's audience makes addressing them much easier (personal communication, May 7, 1991).

These views were corroborated by another physicist, who said:

> I'd say for me now having met most all the people who will read my papers makes a huge difference in how I write them. I don't know if I actually visualize this, but it's like writing or giving a talk to people you know. Before it was like writing an abstract paper and sending it to a journal to be read by abstract people. Earlier on, when you haven't met readers, it's more difficult to have a sense of what real flesh and blood readers will think. It's harder to put it into a broader context. You don't have a sense of the spectrum of perspectives. So, having repeated and continual contact with people [makes it easier to write to them]. (Brad, personal communication, August 21, 1991)

Reflecting further on his experiences in writing to specific audiences in his field, this scientist added,

> I feel I have a much better sense of who might read the article I write. I guess I'd attribute that to *15 years of experience in the field* [emphasis added]—talking with people and developing a sense of what they understand or what we might have to take an extra paragraph to explain. For the most part, right now, the audience would be a pretty well-defined one that I'm familiar with. (Brad, personal communication, August 21, 1991)

Social immersion, then, has as its primary aim initiation into the conversation of one's community. This seems to be as true for newcomers as it is for the experienced professionals who are already well advanced in their careers. In other words, scientific authors, regardless of how experienced they are, interact with their audiences in order to reach them. My findings suggest that this action rule also applies when authors enter the conversation of a new and unfamiliar community.

HOW SCIENTISTS LEARN ABOUT UNFAMILIAR AUDIENCES: INTERACTIONS IN ACROSS- OR NEW-GROUP SITUATIONS

With the DOMC project, the problem of learning about audience became even more difficult as the physicists faced a very different situation from that of addressing members of their own community. In fact, from the start of this project, Swendsen expressed concerns with identifying and address-ing the members of the unfamiliar communities they planned to target. He initially addressed this unfamiliarity, and the uncertainties that attended it, 2 years before the physicists began composing the DOMC paper. In spring 1989, when I was working with Swendsen on another research project, he indicated that he was already concerned about presenting the DOMC work to biologists and chemists. He said that he had not written for or published in their journals, and, as a result, he was not sure how to address them, or what concerns they would have.

Two years later, when the physicists began writing papers on this work, Swendsen expressed these same concerns: "It's not a standard physics audi-ence in this case, so I don't know them well. I'm extrapolating to try to imag-ine what their concerns are, what they think is interesting, mysterious" (personal communication, March 8, 1991). Swendsen said he lacked the same sort of intimate knowledge of biologists' and chemists' day-to-day work or of their concerns in carrying out this work that he had of his physics' colleagues. This lack of knowledge, he believed, would make it more diffi-cult for the physicists to address these other scientists.

When they began the DOMC paper, Swendsen, Bouzida, and Kumar were thus very uncertain about their audiences. To lessen this uncertainty, they relied, as they had in addressing their own community, on various social inputs. In other words, they continued to approach audience analysis as a social enterprise based on direct interactions with actual members of their audiences. For example, some time after they had begun the DOMC paper, Swendsen said that interacting with biologists and chemists had helped him to learn about his audiences in these fields: "I developed a general sense of knowledge of biologists and chemists basically by talking to them. I know [named several individuals], so I can get a little bit of an idea of what they're aware of, what issues they'll think of and what they won't" (personal com-munication, May 21, 1991). Kumar discussed a similar approach: "My sense of what they know comes from my interactions with them. I think I know what they [biologists] know.... They know less physics and mathematics than say chemists" (personal communication, May 14, 1991). [Kumar was situated in a biological sciences department for his postdoctoral fellowship, so he interacted with biologists on a daily basis]. The physicists thus relied on interactions with these members of their audiences to construct their own model of their audience that accounted for their audiences' knowledge, interests, and ongoing work.

Other physicists I interviewed also emphasized the importance of interacting with scientists to learn about unfamiliar communities. For example, one physicist said:

> The analogy for me ... is to go into particle physics.... This has been a tendency for me in the last several years. I now know, or have had to meet, many people ... through the particle group—seminar speakers, etc. Also, at the University of Maryland and Los Alamos. So it's really old fashioned—going to conferences and meeting with people in person. (Len, personal communication, September 6, 1991)

Len said that for him this process, which enabled him to meet and become familiar with numerous particle physicists, lasted for several years (at least 5 or 6). However, Len also acknowledged that he continues to struggle with understanding this community, which reinforces how long it may take to move into a new community, as well as how difficult it may be to maintain a foot in two distinct communities (personal communication, September 6, 1991).

In Len's view, such processes, which he acknowledged are time-consuming, are nonetheless important. Another physicist made a similar point, suggesting the importance of using interactions, initially, to learn what others are doing in a field. He described his own experiences entering a new community by saying:

> I'm getting into work that has more of an applied physics feel to it so my audience is going to change, at least for that work. I have also been doing something similar to Swendsen. I'm doing things differently in a relatively established field that I haven't published papers in. I have used e-mail to make inquiries to see who's doing what.... It's important not to come into a field ignorant of what's gone on, even if you know that an aspect of what you're doing is new and different. (Eric, personal communication, September 6, 1991)

This physicist added as a caution, "You have to avoid saying that people have been awfully stupid and this is the right way to do it," which is something the physicists faced because their claims contradicted well-accepted procedures (Eric, personal communication, September 6, 1991). Len's and Eric's comments reinforce the need for learning, gradually and over time, what is being done in a new community—in short, a process by which across-group socialization may occur.[6] Their comments also suggest that scientists should approach such situations with an openness to the approaches and perspectives of the new communities.

Like these scientists, Swendsen also believed that it was important to understand what the members of his audiences would know and perceive, and what issues they would find significant. He believed that if he, Bouzida, and Kumar were to succeed in persuading these scientists, they needed to understand how biologists and chemists carried out simulations and what concerns they had in undertaking this work. The strategies the physicists used to learn about these concerns included reading the literature in these fields, watching a closed-circuit television program addressing computer simulations, interacting with particular individuals in these communities and then generalizing from these interactions to their larger audience, making assumptions about the members of their audiences based on their group affiliations (or what Krauss and Fussell referred to as category membership), and, finally, positioning themselves as actual members of these communities. However, for time reasons, they also occasionally sought shortcuts to learning about their audiences.

Using the Literature and Other Media to Learn About Audience

Reading the literature was one strategy that Swendsen acknowledged would be very valuable in becoming familiar with these communities. Kumar also addressed this strategy. He said, "just by reading things in their journals.... Then [you] get an idea of their interests, jargon, and, very importantly, what they would understand" (personal communication, April 17, 1991). Kumar said that he makes judgments about what his readers know or don't know based on what he sees them producing in their disciplines (personal communication, April 17, 1991). A genre that is well suited to this activity in science is the review article, which offers broad coverage of the existing research in an area. One physicist I interviewed described these articles by saying, "There are review papers where you review things for people not as versed in your specialty who want an overview. In these you tend to start in general terms or write in largely gory detail" (Rich, personal communication, August 9, 1991). Swendsen also acknowledged the usefulness of such papers, both for obtaining and for providing a comprehensive overview of a field. He said this is why they cited review papers in the early conference paper and then again in the final DOMC paper.

Scholars concerned with genres and discourse communities have also addressed the value of becoming familiar with the literature produced in a field. Park (1982), for example, correlated audience with genres and argued that knowledge of audiences can be derived from written forms. Porter (1992) talked about coming to know one's audience through immersion in the discourse of the community (p. 109). He contended that authors can use such discourse to understand the episteme of the community, the classifying principles, rules of formation and exclusion, and so on (pp. 111–112).[7] He said, "The first goal of the writer is 'socialization' into the community, which requires an understanding of the community's unstated assumptions as well as its explicit conventions and intertextuality" (p. 112).[8]

Although the physicists acknowledged the usefulness of this strategy, they also acknowledged shortcutting it. For example, when Swendsen addressed the value of soliciting input from prospective audience members on what journal to target, he said:

> I don't read their journals. The idea is that we're writing a paper for these people, then we'll take it to the people … who can advise us on a journal. Then they can tell us, but we need to be at a certain point and have things worked out. The only alternative is to spend a lot of time reading those journals. It seems a lot more efficient this way, but we need to give them a pretty good sense of things. (Swendsen, personal communication, May 21, 1991)

Swendsen here chose an alternative time-saving strategy of talking to other scientists, perhaps assuming that it would be sufficient for them to proceed with a general sense of their audiences and then check or verify that sense by having members of their audiences read what they had written. Authors may thus apportion time and attention in particular writing situations, which can have an impact on how ideas are shaped and organized, as well as on outcomes. "Time" is a critical factor in composing. Time is also a resource that engenders gambles, such as it is better to be first with ideas and not perfect with audience, or it is better to wait and be sure to satisfy audience.

Time may have also been a factor in another strategy Swendsen used to learn about the communities he wished to address with this work. In fact, in another effort to save time in obtaining information about their audiences, Swendsen mentioned using another medium to gauge the likely responses and concerns of his readers, a closed-circuit television program that addressed biological simulations. Swendsen described this program and what he learned from watching it by saying:

> There was a closed-circuit course on television about this last year that I viewed.… There was one point where one fellow was asked about the differences between MC and MD and his answer was total nonsense. So, there are things people take as valid. If he is going to believe something like that, there are statements we have to make.… I gained a general idea of attitudes here—what people were trying to calculate, what they regarded as evidence of something being a good way to do things. (Swendsen, personal communication, May 21, 1991)

This source—although somewhat unconventional—provided the physicists with additional, useful information about (a) how members of their audiences might respond to their ideas—what attitudes they might bring to them, and (b) how, therefore, they would need to present those ideas given such attitudes and potential responses (the two operations I identified with the social interaction model that I outlined at the start of the chapter). However, the difficulties the physicists ended up having when they finally addressed their audiences (see chaps. 4 and 5) suggest that knowing the former (a) does not readily lead to the latter (b), which my findings suggest requires skill, feedback, and immersion. Thus, although (a) may come somewhat readily, (b) likely does not; however, rhetorical training often assumes that (b) naturally follows (a) and therefore ignores it. The potential consequences of this, however, are suggested by this case.

There are really two distinct operations, therefore, that need to occur in rhetorical situations such as this one. These include getting to know and understand one's interlocutors and then determining how to influence them. And my case shows how interaction, and the general know-how and ability to interact, are constitutive of both of these operations. Furthermore, my case also shows that the first operation does not automatically lead to the second. Swendsen, Bouzida, and Kumar seemed, in general, to have greater success in accomplishing the former than the latter, which may not be entirely surprising given the complex nature of such operations.

Interacting with Particular Individuals and Generalizing From Those Interactions to the Larger Audience

In addition to familiarizing themselves, at least to a certain extent, with the literature of the domains they were targeting, the physicists also obtained information about their audiences by extrapolating general characteristics of them based on their understanding of a few of the members. In other words, another strategy the physicists relied on to obtain information about their audiences entailed attributing certain characteristics to their larger audience based on attributes of specific individuals with whom they interacted as they wrote the DOMC paper; particular audience members thus served as prompts that invoked the larger audience. Perelman and Olbrechts-Tyteca (1969) addressed this strategy by saying, "The choice of the person who will incarnate a particular audience will often influence the methods used in the argumentation" (p. 40). They also said that who authors choose to incarnate their audiences reveals something about their conception of their audience and the ends they hope to attain with it (p. 40), something that also seemed to be true for the physicists, who, despite their general openness to their audiences, still had certain conceptions of them that they sought to verify (see also chaps. 4 and 5).

One shortcoming of such a strategy, however, is that authors may make decisions and changes in their work based primarily on feedback or input from just a single or a few members of their audience, whose views may or may not represent those of other audience members. Such a strategy also does not account for idiosyncratic responses and viewpoints, such as that which may have occurred with one of the scientists with whom the physicists interacted. The physicists had asked this and two other scientists—all representing the different communities they were targeting—for feedback on one of the DOMC drafts and for advice on where to submit the paper for publication. The responses the physicists received from these scientists were very different from what they expected. One of the scientists, in particular, whose perspective may have been colored at least partly by his personal relationship with Swendsen, had a significant influence on the physicists' overall rhetorical strategy, including who they decided to target with the work and where they decided to submit it for publication. This one scientist's response was thus a key factor in the physicists' eventual decision to redefine their audience so that they were scientists, specifically other physicists, who would be more receptive to their work.

Such a strategy of extrapolating from single interlocutors may have significant consequences, therefore, for authors' rhetorical strategies. In this case, their shift back to physicists as their primary audience was a critical decision, and one that once again underscores the disconnection that may occur between knowing one's audiences, especially when those audiences are new and unfamiliar, and knowing how to gain acceptance as a voice in their conversation or forum.

Making Assumptions About Audience Members Based on Group Affiliation

Another, somewhat similar strategy the physicists relied on to learn about their audiences was one that Krauss and Fussell (1990) called category membership. In this case, this strategy entailed inferring the concerns of audience members based on their disciplinary affiliations. As an example of how the physicists used this strategy, Swendsen once said:

> A couple of things I know about the audience. Biologists ... generally don't have as thorough grounding in statistical mechanics and methods. Chemists probably do have grounding in statistical mechanics but not in simulation methods. Statistical physicists know statistical mechanics and simulation methods.... And the audience I'm speaking to here also has a very clear preference for one method—MD—which is dominant in the field. We're coming along and saying something different. (Swendsen, personal communication, May 7, 1991)

Kumar and Bouzida also made inferences about various scientists based on the disciplines to which they belonged (see the earlier discussion in this chapter of how Bouzida analyzed his audiences for the two presentations he gave). Although the physicists sometimes based their inferences on their interactions with particular individuals, at other times they made assumptions based on their general knowledge of the disciplines.

Such actions are well supported by theorists, some of whom claim that membership in a certain category of a discipline identifies a vocabulary and a body of information that can be assumed to be mutually known (Krauss & Fussell, 1990, p. 140). Bazerman (1985) said that scientists can make predictions based on generalized schema and that individual idiosyncrasies and short-term misunderstandings can be worked out through long-term processes of accumulations—people building on one another's work in the long-term emergence of scientific knowledge (pp. 10, 21). In *Shaping Written Knowledge* (1988), he also said, "Through coming to know how statuses, roles, and relations tend to be structured in a field you can, nevertheless, gain a fairly good idea of your audience" (pp. 325–326). Perelman & Olbrechts-Tyteca (1969) conveyed similar notions when they said that although individuals influence our impression of the group, what we think of the group predisposes us to a particular impression of those who form it (p. 322).

However, such beliefs may also lend further support to conceptualizing scientific audiences as abstractions, as Gross and Prelli and other scholars did, rather than viewing them as sociological entities comprised of diverse individuals with varied viewpoints, perspectives, and backgrounds. In other words, such beliefs may prevent authors from getting a well-developed enough sense of their audiences. Thus, such a strategy may also entail potential consequences because it operates at too high a level of generality. Coupled with other strategies it may be productive, but taken alone it may be insufficient. The strength of this strategy is that it provides a sort of universal scientific "shorthand." However, a limitation, and a rather serious one, is that it may preclude the sort of well-developed understanding that Swendsen described earlier: when "you know when all you have to do is wave your hand versus driving something very hard" (personal communication, May 7, 1991). Authors end up lacking knowledge in such situations of how interactions with audience members are likely to go. Additionally, familiarity allows an author to address and write to an audience with ease because he or she knows the majority of the members of the audience personally. Finally, longer term immersion and face-to-face interaction with actual members of a domain can push authors past stereotypical positionings.

Locating Themselves in the Communities They Were Targeting

A final strategy the physicists used to learn about their audiences in biology and chemistry entailed having Kumar and Bouzida cross into and actually become members of these communities. This strategy illustrates how graduate students and postdoctoral fellows can function as boundary spanners between their own and other communities. In particular, Kumar already held a postdoctoral fellowship position in a biological sciences department, and, as I finished my research, Bouzida obtained one in a biomedical engineering research center. The physicists expressed three objectives in seeking direct membership in these communities: (1) gaining additional knowledge about these communities and about the problems that members of them were interested in studying; (2) obtaining a greater understanding of the work carried out in these other communities; and (3) increasing the likelihood of having their work read and accepted by these scientists. In other words, Swendsen, Kumar, and Bouzida believed that by entering and working in these other areas directly they could gain increased acceptance of themselves and of their work, as well as acquire a better understanding of the areas. As Swendsen said:

> Biologists and chemists are interested in different questions and validity checks.... It will be a two-way educational process. We have to learn what's important to them and what's important in the biological properties of the chemicals. This is the reason Djamal is looking for positions with people in those communities who do this. He'll learn a lot more about the biochemistry of these things and will be able to carry his work a lot further. He doesn't know much chemistry and biology, but he knows a lot more than most of them about simulating these molecules. (Swendsen, personal communication, March 1, 1991)

The physicists believed that by situating themselves in the communities they were targeting they could facilitate ongoing and two-way interactions with their constituents. The DOMC research did enough, then, to land both of these scientists positions in these "new" groups.

In commenting on his own perceptions of and experiences with these strategies, Bouzida expressed views similar to Swendsen's. Regarding his search for a postdoctoral post, he indicated that he needed to know more about biological and chemical systems, and "The only way I can do this is by being a postdoc. For example, working with Beveridge and working with protein and DNA interactions" (personal communication, March 1, 1991). After obtaining and starting his position, Bouzida also addressed the importance of immersion in and exposure to an area, which he said was helping him to learn the language of the area and to become socialized into it (his comments echo the sentiments of the physicists and scholars cited earlier):

> I'm surrounded by molecular biologists.... You're coming in from a different area and all you know about biology is what you've read in books and you feel

like you're learning fast. In fact, I am learning fast. I can speak their language. It's been only two months. Not the details but the important stuff, the important stuff biologists usually talk about. I'm still a statistical physicist of course. (personal communication, November 16, 1991)

Bouzida's comments about speaking their language are especially interesting in light of his struggles, which he was experiencing at the same time, with learning the language in his own community.

In discussing these issues, Bouzida also addressed the value of being able to interact with these scientists on a regular basis. Although his comments in this regard may have been prompted by his awareness of my interests for the study, he acknowledged the importance of this daily interaction as a means of monitoring and keeping track of his constituents' concerns:

I also interact with the people here, so I can stop by any office and talk about ideas.... I think I'm learning a lot more about biology right now. I want to learn more biology and interact with people from a different background, and know better my audience, huh? That was the whole objective of the postdoc. (personal communication, November 16, 1991)

Kumar expressed a similar sense of using his postdoc to learn and understand his constituents, "I'm in an office in a biological sciences department.... I think I know what they know" (personal communication, May 14, 1991).

The physicists' concerns with positioning themselves in the communities they were targeting also suggest the ongoing nature of their efforts to learn about and understand their audiences. Each of the physicists in my study was concerned with fostering ongoing relationships with members of their audiences and with not restricting such encounters to a single rhetorical episode, or even to one part of such an episode. Rather, they felt the need to participate directly in these communities and to engage in ongoing interactions. In their minds, such activities would help them both to further develop their conceptions of their audiences and to improve their persuasive efforts. Their actions show an awareness of both the immediate and the longer term contexts for their work.

CONCLUSION

In contrast to what Perelman & Olbrechts-Tyteca and other scholars have occasionally suggested, audience for the physicists was far from a transparent or unproblematic phenomenon. These scientists expended a great deal of energy learning about and developing knowledge structures of both their familiar and their unfamiliar audiences that would hopefully assist them as they planned for and then publicly presented their work—through multiple social inputs and strategies, the physicists acquired and constructed a general store of knowledge about their audiences, which they used as they prepared their work for dissemination.

Audience, for the physicists, came to mean real people with whom they would engage and interact over the course of their research and writing processes, and even beyond. Although audiences are complex, dynamic entities that can never be known completely, and thus, of necessity, entail some level of abstraction, they are also real entities that can be addressed and made more concrete and discernible. Such findings suggest that it may be much more productive to think of authors' understanding of and approaches to audience as resting on a continuum someplace between imagined and real, rather than as being exclusively one or the other. [9]

The physicists often worked from an abstract conceptualization, but that conceptualization was based on their knowledge and understanding of real people. In other words, audience for the physicists was sometimes abstract, but at other times it was a concrete, physically present reality that influenced them as they composed and positioned their texts. As Selzer (1992) said, "Writer and audience and text are inextricably patterned in the creation of meaning through discourse" (p. 173). Audience is thus an integrated, and integral, component of an author's larger rhetorical process, and learning about audience entails a dynamic process: Successful writers continually adjust their strategies and negotiate and adapt to barriers and opportunities posed by their interlocutors. Doing this, realistically, may entail certain trade-offs—for example, particular writing situations can pose significant time constraints, which often are not addressed in our writing classes.

All of these responses to audience by the physicists also suggest the significance of the actions of authors, as well as of their interlocutors, in constructing, assessing, and using knowledge of audiences. Actions are what make the repeatable behaviors we label as, for instance, "considering your audience." Therefore, actions, and not the labels for those actions, or the labels for the purported causes or conditions of actions, are what is key: Possessing the label does not cause the action; rather, the action and the knowledge attained through the action (e.g., firsthand knowledge of what members of one's audiences know and believe) are what make the label, and the behaviors it signifies, important.

By examining actions, and the local contexts in which they occur, researchers in rhetoric can better understand various behaviors, such as learning about audience. The physicists' actions in learning about their audiences for the DOMC paper suggest to us the value of social encounters with interlocutors, especially for newcomers to a field, and the value of finding new opportunities for and maintaining such encounters throughout one's career. Their actions also reveal the uncertainties authors may experience in addressing various audiences, along with the instability of authors' knowledge of and representations of their audiences. The uncertainties the physicists experienced became apparent even before they started composing the DOMC paper, and they persisted beyond the paper's publication.

Writing is a social process that involves envisioned as well as real, interactionally experienced audiences. As my data in this chapter illustrate, authors' interactions with audiences are affected by such issues as time and efficiency; willingness and capability to change; ethos and status; genre and type of acceptance sought; duration and intensity or depth of experience within one's own or a different community; and inherent skill. These constraints also figure prominently in the next two chapters. My findings also suggest the importance of interaction for both knowing one's audience and knowing how to reach and influence that audience, especially when it is not in the same community as the author. The physicists seemed to have a better grasp of the former than the latter, which the next two chapters also illustrate.

NOTES

1. Some of the information authors need to obtain about their audiences includes a sense of what audience members know, how they know it, how they construct and view the field, how they read and interpret the field's literature, what they believe, why they hold those beliefs, and how those beliefs influence how they approach and interpret the problems of and work in the field. Authors need to be conscious of the individuals they address and of the dominant intellectual beliefs and values of those individuals. How authors develop that consciousness, both in relation to audiences in their own fields and in relation to audiences in other fields, is the primary focus of this chapter.

2. See also Winsor (1996) and Doheny-Farina (1992). Winsor found that the student engineers she studied developed an understanding of their audiences though direct contact with them in work situations, and through exposure to and familiarity with their field's genres. Doheny-Farina also addressed how writers become socialized into communities by learning the assumptions and conventions of the communities.

3. Ong (1975) corroborated Swendsen's views, although in the context of his concerns with thinking of audiences as fictionalized constructs, when he said: "It takes time to get a feel for the roles that readers can be expected comfortably to play in the modern academic world" (p. 19). Krauss and Fussell (1990) likewise noted that "Workers within the same disciplinary area ... are likely to have direct knowledge of one another, either from interactions at previous meetings or from having read each others' publications" (p. 140).

4. See also Brandt (1990) and Haas (1994) who suggested that newcomers and novices are generally less audience aware. Haas hypothesized that students in science are more likely to encounter, engage in, and develop rhetorical awareness through reading prior to developing domain-specific rhetorical awareness in writing (p. 47). In other words, students in science usually are not exposed directly to members of their audiences—in this case other scientists in their community—until they engage in actual projects with their advisors during the latter stages of their graduate work. Acquiring knowledge of one's community, therefore, is a process that just begins in graduate school.

5. On the other hand, it may have resulted from other factors as well, such as the power relations that typically exist between professors and graduate students, and even, at times, between professors and their colleagues. At Bouzida's thesis defense, which was attended by chemists and biologists, as well as physicists, the same lack of order and antagonism seemed to exist as in the physics lunch talk. I was later told by both Swendsen and Bob, another outside informant, that such responses are not typical and that they may have been caused by interpersonal disagreements and controversies among the scientists in attendance.

6. It may be important to note here that the socialization process, described by scholars like Porter (1992) and Doheny-Farina (1992), may not be the same as what scientists like Swendsen undergo. The physicists did not want to become biologists and chemists. They simply wanted to get to know and persuade these scientists (they were more concerned with gathering specific information than with becoming completely socialized). The physicists were also trying to learn about biologists and chemists, but not vice versa. They wanted these scientists to want to know about DOMC, but they had to create that interest. There was a sense, in other words, in which a mutual shaping and reshaping did not occur here—it was more of a one-way adaptation. However, despite this, and despite their not wanting to be completely socialized, the physicists suggested through their comments the value of a certain amount of exposure to, and immersion in, these communities.

7. Porter (1992) proposed a heuristic called forum analysis, which consists of questions writers can use to explore the forums they are trying to enter (p. 112). This analysis, Porter said, is a kind of textual analysis that focuses writer's attention on discursive practices rather than imagined "real readers" (pp. 137–138). The heuristic assumes that audience is defined by the texts it produces and that the writer needs to explore this textual field in order to produce acceptable discourse (p. 112). It sees documents existing in a field of already established practices and consists of developing an awareness of how planned discourses will fit into the existing network of discursive practices (p. 141), an awareness, in other words, of the discursive field one is entering (p. 142).

8. Also noteworthy here is Selzer's (1992) observation that discourse communities are broader than audiences—particular audiences, he said, exist within discourse communities (p. 172). Selzer noted, also, that many members of a discourse community will not be among the intended or implied real audiences for a document (p. 172).

9. Scholars in rhetoric have addressed audience from a number of perspectives. Two common ones, which are often even presented as being exclusive of each other, include thinking of audiences as fictionalized, or discursive constructs created by authors (imagined or implied readers), and thinking of them as actual, sociological entities who actively engage in the processes of interpreting and making meaning (intended or real readers), (Ede & Lunsford, 1984). [Porter (1992) connected these conceptions to reader-response criticism and to its concerns with what happens after a text is written—in particular, with responses to literary texts and with problems associated with the reader role in literary criticism (pp. 72–73).] Numerous scholars in rhetorical studies have theorized and applied these perspectives. Some of the scholars who treat audiences as fictionalized or discursive constructs include Gragson and Selzer (1990), Long (1980, 1990), McCloskey (1985), Ong (1975), and White (1985), and some of those who conceptualize audiences as external sociological realities are Berkenkotter (1981), Elbow (1987), Kirsch & Roen (1990), Park (1982), Rafoth (1989), Roen & Willey (1988), Roth (1987), and Selzer (1992). Brandt (1990) summarized these various treatments of audience in rhetoric, saying:

> Rhetoric and composition treat audience more directly from a writer's viewpoint but, even so, from a wide range of perspectives: from literal views of a preexisting, demographic audience ... to more sophisticated versions, such as Douglas Park's, which present audience as a set of interests that can be aroused by the moves that a text makes. (p. 69)

However, few scholars in the field have tested these notions empirically by examining, through firsthand observations of authors composing, like mine, how authors, situated in communities of practice among heterogeneous coactors, deal with and address their audiences as they engage in actual rhetorical activities within the context of these communities (vs. inferring this information from already completed texts), (for some exceptions see Johnson, 1997; Schriver, 1997; Spilka, 1988a, 1988b, 1990).

4

Following the DOMC Text Into Communal Interactive Dynamics: Authors Getting to Know and Interacting With Audiences in Real Practice

Chapter 3 showed how functional knowledge of audience comes only over time by interacting with the actual members of one's audience, whereas this and the following chapter show the potential effects of this interaction on scientists' writing and research. In these next two chapters, I look at Swendsen's, Bouzida's, and Kumar's overt attempts to get feedback on the DOMC text from specific members of their audiences. I examine what that feedback was and how they responded to it. Specifically, I follow the physicists' DOMC text into communal interactive dynamics, telling what the authors did to get to know and interact with specific members of their audiences in real practice and with what consequences. I show them interacting with and coming to know (and be influenced by) three members of their audiences on a direct and personal level.

Generally, my findings in these two chapters provide a concrete sense of how authors may interact with audiences to learn more about them and also of how authors may respond to such interactions. What the findings I present in these chapters do not provide is an independent view of the three audience members' readings outside of their comments; a view of their responses to the changes the physicists made in response to their feedback; or a sense of other readers in the field to see if the scientists who reviewed the physicists' work were typical, to judge the depth and extent of their perspectives, or to get at other perceptions of what was at stake in the difficulties to which they pointed.

As a result of the feedback they received from their interactions with these audience members, the physicists ended up taking several actions that they might not have otherwise taken. In this chapter I show how the physicists came to alter their publication strategy to target members of their own discipline with the DOMC paper rather than biologists and chemists. In the next chapter I show ways in which the physicists altered specific parts of the DOMC text in response to these audience members' comments. My findings in both of these chapters show how such processes of interacting with real audiences are gradual, and sometimes even limited. Specifically, in looking at the physicists' interactions with these scientists I get at the limits and extensiveness of the physicists' actions both in relation to their own goals, as well as in relation to the goals and actions of specific members of their audiences.

SOLICITING INPUT FROM COLLEAGUES

Winsor (1996) argued in her book for viewing audiences as active interpreters of texts and as comembers of communities engaged in negotiating the meaning of texts (p. 45). The interactive and recursive relationships that she said writers have with their readers (as opposed to the unidirectional or temporally limited ones suggested by more static conceptions of audience; p. 4[1]) resemble the relationships the physicists developed with some of their readers as they composed the DOMC paper. Specifically, after the physicists produced 13 drafts of the DOMC paper, and when they felt that they had a well-developed and polished version of the paper, they decided to solicit feedback from specific members of their audiences. Doing this, they said, would hopefully give them additional information about their readers —they were ready to test the generalized assumptions about their audiences that they said had been guiding their work to this point. They also hoped that feedback from actual audience members would assist them as they prepared the final drafts of the paper. When he discussed this strategy initially, Swendsen said, "We really need advice from Ken, David, and George" (Swendsen, review meeting for draft 1 of the DOMC paper, March 5, 1991). David, a biophysicist, and George, a chemist, were Swendsen's colleagues at Carnegie Mellon University, whereas Ken, a biologist, was Kumar's supervisor for his postdoctoral position.

When the physicists distributed the paper to these scientists, Swendsen said that he and Bouzida and Kumar had done what they could to anticipate the likely concerns of their readers. They expected, primarily, requests to clarify information so that it would better address the concerns of their audiences. They also expected straightforward advice on where to publish the DOMC paper. In describing the responses he anticipated from these scientists, Swendsen said:

> We'll possibly get challenges from them. They don't believe some things.... Possibly clarifications, possibly requests for more information to back up some things.... Things we might think are obvious that they don't. I don't know what; I've tried to anticipate.... Also, things we've learned over the past few years that we now regard as obvious. There might be biological or chemical statements where we've made a mistake, or we may have used a form, words, or phrases that would be clear to a physicist but not to a biologist or chemist. (personal communication, May 21, 1991)

David, the biophysicist, expressed similar ideas about audience input. He said that giving a paper to colleagues or to other scientists is especially useful for identifying problems that authors might otherwise overlook: "As an author, there are incredible blind spots involved. You just don't see things. A well-known strategy is ... what Swendsen did, have a colleague read it. That's a good way to avoid problems" (personal communication, June 7, 1991). Perelman and Olbrechts-Tyteca (1969) also addressed this strategy: "It also very often happens that discussion with someone else is simply a means we use to see things more clearly ourselves" (p. 41).

The physicists thus anticipated that the feedback from these exchanges would help them to address concerns that biologists and chemists might have with the work. They did not expect to be considered wrong, but they did acknowledge that they might receive certain challenges to the work. In this case, those challenges were tied both to the physicists' strategies for positioning the DOMC work and to the manner in which they had situated and presented their claims. Because of these challenges, the physicists ended up rethinking their audiences for the DOMC paper, their plans for publishing it, and even the issue of what constitutes sufficient evidence in these different communities. My examinations of these scientists' feedback, and of the physicists' responses to it, reinforce that the processes of learning about audiences, as well as about what matters in a field, are complex, social ones that occur only gradually and that are also sometimes limited.

SEEKING AND RESPONDING TO ADVICE ON WHERE TO PUBLISH THE DOMC PAPER

During the early stages of my research, when the physicists were just beginning the DOMC paper, they said that their primary audiences for the paper were biologists and chemists and that they would publish it in one of these field's journals. However, they were not yet sure which one. Bouzida said,

"The audience is going to be biologists and chemists.... Actually, this is a new method, and you want to get as many people as possible to read it and under-stand it" (personal communication, March 18, 1991). On another occasion, he said, "When I wrote this [one of the DOMC drafts] I was thinking about the *Journal of Chemical Physics*. So the audience will be chemists, but also biol-ogists and physicists" (personal communication, March 7, 1991).

During this early stage, Swendsen also expressed his sense of who they were writing to and where he thought the physicists should publish the pa-per. From his perspective, the journals in their own field (*Physical Review* and *Physical Review Letters*), although options, were probably not where they would send it:

> I don't think *Physical Review Letters* is the right place for this. We could put it in *Physical Review*, but that will hide it from chemistry.... Or we could do both—set up for different systems. The same general ideas but applied to dif-ferent systems ... and place it in different journals. We want one that's willing to look at not new results, but methods. (Swendsen, review meeting for draft 1 of the DOMC paper, March 5, 1991)

Two comments in this excerpt eventually became significant. First, Swendsen suggests the possibility of publishing the DOMC work in differ-ent places—of essentially splitting it up based on applications and placing it in different journals. This is the strategy the physicists ultimately ended up employing. Swendsen also notes in his comments that the focus of the DOMC paper is primarily on methods, a factor that also became significant in the physicists' final decision on where to publish the paper.

One of their most important concerns, then, when they gave the DOMC paper to Ken, David, and George to review was figuring out where to publish it: "Now the most important thing is getting advice on what journal we're going to put it in and what we need to do from here" (Swendsen, personal communication, March 21, 1991). Swendsen also expressed his belief that members of these communities would offer them the best advice on this: "The idea is that we're writing a paper for these people, then we'll take it to the people ... who can advise us on the journal" (personal communication, May 21, 1991). Swendsen' comments seem consistent with those expressed by Law (1986), who also addressed journal selection in science from the per-spective of audience:

> First there is the question of *where* scientists choose to send their texts or, more precisely at *whom* or *what* the texts are aimed. This requires that we step outside the text itself and consider negotiations about the journals to which texts might be submitted, negotiations that are organized around conceptions of the interests of possible audiences. (pp. 67–68)

When physicists publish in their own field, usually they choose between *Physical Review Letters*, which publishes relatively short articles featuring novel findings, and *Physical Review*, a more archival journal comprised of several parts that correspond to the major subfields in physics. These two journals are the leading American journals in the discipline, and they also have strong international reputations (Blakeslee, 1994; Merton & Zuckerman, 1973). Physicists feel confident about publishing in them. Among other things, they know their readers: Swendsen actually has met and has a substantial history of interactions with most of the physicists working in his area. He once said, "If I put it in a physics journal like *Physical Review Letters*, then people I know will read it" (personal communication, May 21, 1991). He added that publishing in the journals of other fields, in contrast, carries greater uncertainty: "I don't know what will happen with these journals because I don't have any experience with them" (personal communication, May 21, 1991).

However, Swendsen also expressed faith in the system. When he discussed the prospect of publishing the DOMC paper in a biology or chemistry journal, he said, "I don't think we'll have any trouble if the journals are reasonable. I expect they'll request that we reference this or that paper" (personal communication, May 21, 1991). Swendsen's perceptions seem to match those of scholars who view scientific research articles as part of an ordered system (Bazerman, 1988; Blakeslee, 1994; Crane, 1972; Garvey, 1979; Kronick, 1976; Latour, 1987; Merton & Zuckerman, 1973; Price, 1986; Swales, 1990). What these scholars do not address, however, is what happens when scientists publish outside of their fields. Knorr (1979) pointed out that, "Contrary to what we might think, criteria of 'what matters' and 'what does not matter' are neither fully defined nor standardized throughout the scientific community; nor are the rules of official science exempted from local interpretation" (p. 361). For his part, Swendsen expected the reviewers and editors of these publications to be reasonable, at least according to his sense of what reasonable means in scientific publishing; however, the feedback he received from David and George, in particular, lead him to wonder whether his notion of reasonableness applied in this situation. This feedback also made him question whether it was even wise to publish in these journals.

Although each of the three scientists recommended specific journals to the physicists, what these journals were and why they recommended them surprised the physicists. One of the scientists, David, even advised that they publish the DOMC paper in *Physical Review*, which contradicted everything the physicists had thought of doing up to this point. When he discussed this advice in an interview, David said he based it on the content of the DOMC paper. The physicists were concerned in this paper, primarily, with establishing the efficiency of the DOMC method. They were not concerned with presenting particular applications of the method; that would come later (see the earlier discussion, in chap. 2, of how they defined their research problem). David addressed these concerns, and their impact on his recommendation, saying:

> It comes down to the content of the paper. My impression of what he's doing in the paper comes from the title, "efficient methods." ... There's the question of where you publish proof of method and does it differ, and I think it does, from where you publish results or application. Proof belongs in more physics journals. Applications in biological journals. My sense was this was more a methods paper. (personal communication, June 7, 1991)

David also explained that he made this recommendation based on his conceptions of what the physicists' audiences would find interesting.[2] He said:

> The SHO [simple harmonic oscillator] is a simple problem to show the method works. This is appropriate, but not necessarily interesting to someone reading a biological journal. I think it would be appropriate for a particular section of *Physical Review* publishing papers on biological systems. It would be reaching the other hard-core simulators, many of whom are physicists. It would not be reaching those working with proteins, but would it really tell them anything? They're interested in application. I would publish it in a journal where the referees would be able to recognize the technical components. [It would be] better in *Physical Review* than [in the] *Journal of Molecular Biology*. (personal communication, June 7, 1991)

Swendsen, Bouzida, and Kumar acknowledged that the DOMC paper was a methods paper, but they did not think they needed to publish it in *Physical Review* because of this. In David's opinion, however, biologists and chemists probably would not be interested in the methodological aspects of the work; instead, they would be more interested in applications, which the physicists could provide later. David also said that a physics audience would be better able than a biology or chemistry audience to judge the technical merit of Swendsen's methodological work (personal communication, June 7, 1991).

The chemist with whom the physicists interacted also said the paper should be targeted to an audience interested primarily in methods. However, George recommended a journal in his own field: "I believe the better place for submission of this paper might be the *Journal of Computational Chemistry* since it is so algorithm oriented" (e-mail communication to Djamal Bouzida, June 6, 1991). When he discussed this suggestion in my interview with him, George said that he based it on both the content of the paper and the quality of the physicists' work, which he criticized:

The *Journal of Computational Physics* is a high quality journal. This isn't good enough or high enough quality of science. The *Journal of Computational Chemistry* is a solid journal which publishes a large number of papers on algorithms, but not at the same level. (personal communication, June 17, 1991)

George also described the audience the work would then reach: "Who it would reach would be potentially people like myself. People developing algorithms and studying biophysical processes. There is a growing community of that ilk" (personal communication, June 17, 1991).

George's suggestion, in some respects, seemed consistent with the physicists' intentions, which were to publish the DOMC paper in a biology or chemistry journal. However, George also indicated that he would have found the DOMC paper problematic had he reviewed it (he expressed this concern to me in an interview and to the physicists in an e-mail message he sent to Bouzida):

If I had reviewed this, it would have been a problem. The review process is very, very, very variable. Some pay less attention to those things. And sometimes it depends on how far out of the field the people are.... If I had gotten it there would have been problems. (personal communication, June 17, 1991)

These comments suggested to Swendsen that biologists and chemists might misunderstand, misinterpret, or even not appreciate the work, outcomes the physicists had hoped to avoid through their early and gradual positioning of the work (see chap. 2).

As a result of both David's and George's responses, Swendsen, Bouzida, and Kumar ended up questioning several aspects of their work. They questioned who they were trying to reach with the DOMC paper, what they were trying to argue in the paper, how the different communities would receive and respond to the paper, and whether biologists and chemists would ever even read and accept it. Part of the exchange in which they began addressing these concerns follows:

Swendsen: I asked where to put it, and he [David] said *Physical Review.*

Kumar: Ken [the biologist] says *Biopolymers* because this is mainly for the biological community, which doesn't read *Physical Review....*

Swendsen: David said publish a methods paper in *Physical Review* and an application paper in a biology or chemistry journal....

Kumar: Then we have to write a different paper. We dismissed *Physical Review* a long time ago because you said you wanted it to reach a different audience. Ken said *Biopolymers, Biopoly-*

> *mers* is good. Also, *Journal of Computational Physics* and *Journal of Computational Biology.*

Swendsen: We really could have done this for *Physical Review* without changing it much.

Kumar: Why did David say it should go to *Physical Review?*

Swendsen: He said there's some question about the reference standards of *Physical Chemistry*, and ... *Physical Review* has a biophysics section. It's not always in there though, and I don't read it myself. It's an interesting strategy he's suggesting. He said one argument is that the biologists won't understand the method in great detail. The chemists will—some—but the quality of the journal will make a difference.

Kumar: You are right. The biological community will not understand it. If you wanted me to put a number on it, I'd say 99%.

Swendsen: His point was that they'd be more likely to believe it in *Physical Review*, which is valid. (review meeting for drafts 12, 13, & 14 of the DOMC paper, June 4, 1991)

Although the physicists had not intended to publish the DOMC paper in *Physical Review*, they now saw some merit in this option; however, it also led them to question who they were really trying to address with the paper:

Swendsen: I'm just thinking about the argument from David, and I'm wondering. Who are we aiming at in this first paper most specifically?

Bouzida: Chemists.

Kumar: Chemists and biologists.

Swendsen: The ones who do the simulations. We're aiming at Brooks, McCammon, Kollman, Beveridge [names several scientists who do this kind of work]. (review meeting for drafts 12, 13, & 14 of the DOMC paper, June 4, 1991)

None of the scientists Swendsen named here was a physicist. Therefore, although seeing some value in the approach, they also continued to be concerned about it.

Swendsen, in particular, debated this strategy. Although he seemed to be leaning toward following it in the review meeting, he expressed his reservations about it in an interview with me after the meeting:

> His idea would be part of a strategy of publishing some parts in *Physical Review*, and others on applications in biological journals. This is a new strategy. It's

not one we've been pursuing. I've got to think about it. I'm not happy about *Physical Review* though. It's the wrong audience, the wrong people. David's argument is that though they don't read it initially, they do when it's called to their attention, and this will lend authority to it eventually. (Swendsen, personal communication, June 5, 1991)

Swendsen's primary concern was that they would not reach their intended audiences if they published in *Physical Review*. However, his consideration of George's concerns also made this option appealing. He said, "I'm worried about people reading it from a different perspective, reading it expecting something else, not coming to it on its own terms" (personal communication, June 5, 1991). He added that physicists would "understand what this is about—that we're developing a new method and what the steps are when you develop a new method" (personal communication, June 5, 1991). Swendsen also reflected on the different approaches biologists and chemists take in this work and on his concerns with those approaches (see chap. 2 for the discussion of these differences): "You can't just start off applying something to a big problem [as they do in chemistry and biology].... Start out small and simple. That's the way it's done in the physics community" (personal communication, June 5, 1991).

The like-mindedness of the *Physical Review* audience was thus becoming attractive to Swendsen: "*Physical Review*, I'm thinking of it. I'm thinking of it rather strongly" (personal communication, June 5, 1991). Swendsen wanted to target an audience that would understand the work and be receptive to it. When he addressed these concerns 1 month later, he said, "Maybe the correct audience for this stage is the one that reads *Physical Review*. I think they'll understand what we're doing—why we're doing small systems, testing it in certain ways, and that stuff. We can publish applications, then, in those journals—large systems" (personal communication, July 30, 1991). The physicists' original concerns with the different approaches biologists and chemists take in performing the simulations were once again significant.

Swendsen, Bouzida, and Kumar decided to publish the DOMC paper finally in *Physical Review*. They also decided to follow it up with papers on applications that they would publish in biology and chemistry journals. Swendsen commented on and justified this decision, saying:

Physical Review is not directly reaching our audience. It's changing access to our audience. Everyone has access to *Physical Review*. They just don't read it immediately. Our strategy would be different—get two or three articles in print and then get into applications, and somewhere along the way convince the people in biology and chemistry to read the physics articles, which I still hope would be written in a way they could read. (Swendsen, personal communication, June 5, 1991)

In their revised publication strategy, the physicists would rely on multiple texts (along with presentations[3]) to persuade their readers (biologists and chemists, as well as physicists) of the value of their approach. Rather than accomplish this through a single publication, the physicists decided to develop a series of articles and presentations that would not only substantiate their methodological approach, but also show how it could be applied. They would reference the DOMC paper in these later articles so that biologists and chemists who wished to do so could go back and read it.

The physicists' revised publication strategy was also consistent with David's and George's perceptions of what the physicists needed to do for the DOMC work to have an impact. When I asked David what impact he thought this work would eventually have, he said, "The impact by itself will be very little. It will be the follow-ups that have impact, but you have to establish the method first.... My guess is that to have an impact they need to go out and have applications" (personal communication, June 7, 1991). Responding to this same question, George said:

> If they take these methods, there are sort of two routes that lead to high impact of something that has potential like this. One route involves packaging these kinds of methods and making them available to the community.... Hence, impact is gained through widespread usage and familiarity by people through their use of the methods. Another common route is the use of a given set of techniques or methods to do highly significant problems or applications, in which case the methods will gain acceptance and widespread impact by virtue of the problems that have been solved with them. (personal communication, June 17, 1991)

Swendsen also emphasized the applications when he discussed what would determine finally whether their audiences—biologists and chemists in particular—would accept the DOMC work. He said, "The ultimate test is experimentation—what actually happens.... What we're describing has a testable reality. That is what will ultimately convince people that it's valid" (personal communication, June 3, 1991). He added that how the DOMC paper was written would also determine "whether it makes it into the hands of the people who will use it. [They] can't use it if it's obscure" (personal communication, June 3, 1991).

The physicists' eventual strategy for positioning their work also resembled the argumentative strategies some scholars in rhetoric have addressed. For example, Myers (1996) said we should begin, "seeing texts within linked systems that define possibilities for action and are defined by action" (p. 9). Myers (1990) contended that "The fate of a claim is not decided when it is published ... it depends on who reads it, how it is read, and how it is used" (p. 100). He added that the way a text enters the literature is crucial in determining the eventual status of the claim (p. 96), and the success or failure of a claim seldom hinges on a single paper (p. 98). The physicists' strategy also illustrates one of the important contributions that actor network theory makes to rhetoric: Namely, this theory encourages rhetorical scholars to view the processes leading to the acceptance or rejection of scientists' ideas in terms of multiple and fluid systems. Such systems entail much more than a single, isolated rhetorical act. This theory also encourages a perspective that supports viewing audience members as active consumers and that legitimates authors' efforts to strategically position their work to attain allies for it.

Finally, the physicists' strategy also bears similarities to Perelman and Olbrechts-Tyteca's (1969) discussion of the possibility of splitting an argument into several stages, with stopping points along the way that indicate partial ends (pp. 281–282). In this situation, the different publications would conceivably function as these various stages. These scholars also said that behind this strategy is the idea of breaking up a problem in order to make acceptable a solution that at first sight seems disagreeable: "Once a first stage is passed, the interlocutors find themselves facing a new configuration of the situation which modifies their attitude toward the final issue" (p. 282).[4] Thus, the physicists' objectives for the DOMC paper began to resemble their objectives for the early conference paper—positioning this work to begin obtaining support for it.

In response to these three readers' feedback, the physicists altered their primary audience for the DOMC paper, as well as their strategies for reaching their audiences more generally. They also altered specific aspects of their presentation, including the support they were offering for their claims and their manner of situating and differentiating their work from other work in the field, as shown in the next chapter.

NOTES

1. In general, scholars in composition have tended to view audience primarily from the perspective of authors and the texts they create. Brandt (1990), for example, noted that rhetoric and composition scholars treat audience more directly from the writer's viewpoint than from that of the audience itself (p. 69). Two of the more common conceptions of audience in rhetoric (implied and ideal, or model, readers) exemplify such treatments (with implied readers, writers use textual conventions to embody a role for readers to play, and with ideal readers, writers use a particular construct of readers to generate their texts) (p. 69). Myers (1996) also addressed how rhetoric has tended to view audiences in terms of the controlling powers of producers of texts rather than as agents who actively construct meaning and who place texts in terms of their daily lives (p. 21). Myers said, "It is harder for rhetoricians to deal with the constructive power of consumers who may take a text into new contexts, play with it, ironicize it, reproduce it" (p. 21).

Most rhetorical perspectives on audiences thus conceptualize these entities as passive consumers of the information directed toward them. Such perspectives fail to capture the potential agency of audiences. Porter (1992) argued that such passive conceptions of audience stem from Aristotle, who viewed audience as a receptor of the meaning discovered by the rhetor (p. 15). In this conception, he said, the rhetor was knowledgeable and the audience was ignorant (p. 18). Further, the rhetor was in a position of authority and control over the audience, which would end up waiting to be persuaded (p. 19). This perspective, Porter claimed, allowed for and resulted in our eventual neglect of audience, especially in expressivist and current-traditional rhetorics (p. 19): "Rhetoric developed historically as a discipline empowering the speaker at the expense of the audience. The audience became an object for analysis, worked on and shaped by the speaker" (p. 25). Within such views, authors make distant guesses about audience based on assumptions about uniformity or broad-stroke characterizations aimed at manipulation and domination rather than cooperative interaction. Audiences are portrayed as static, monolithic entities, and influence and persuasion are portrayed primarily in unidirectional terms.

2. Recall the physicists' discussion, earlier (chaps. 1 and 2), of how biologists and chemists would be more interested in complex problems and large molecules.

3. In addition to the published DOMC paper, the physicists realized that they also needed to promote the work though other forums, especially invited talks and conference presentations. As a result, they gave talks both prior to and well past the appearance of the paper in *Physical Review*. They presented the work at conferences in each of the communities they were targeting (e.g., a few months after the paper was published Bouzida did a poster presentation for a conference attended primarily by biologists and chemists), and they also gave several invited talks in biology and chemistry departments at various institutions. Their approach was consistent with David's contention that persuading their audiences would entail more than

> just papers. They have to get out and talk about it.... Just publishing a paper will have little impact. You have to get others to look at it, hear about it, etc.... The way it works now I think you need both—talks and papers in conjunction. People who publish good solid papers but don't give talks don't do as well. Talks act as filters—to filter out or actually filter in that part of the literature you want to look at. So, talks are important in the ultimate impact of all this. (personal communication, June 7, 1991)

4. Bazerman (1988) also addressed the persuasive process that finally took shape in this situation:

> Persuasion, rather than being a single, sudden event, can be a lengthy process of negotiation, transformation, and growth of the central formulations and related arguments. Formulations survive only by entering the living body of scientific activity, influencing behavior, cognition, social relationships, future experience, and new formulations. (p. 308)

5

Interacting With Audience Members: Authors Evaluating and Responding to Audience Feedback[a]

Myers (1990), Knorr-Cetina (1981), and Berkenkotter and Huckin (1995), among others, described how final versions of scientific articles emerge from a kind of negotiation with reviewers that occurs during the revision and acceptance process. The comments that Swendsen, Bouzida, and Kumar received from their heterogeneous readers required a similar kind of re-visioning of their paper. In response to the feedback that David, the biophysicist, gave on a graph, the physicists generated additional data and evidence to support their arguments. Ken, the biologist, generally agreed with the physicists' presentation; therefore, his feedback did not elicit any substantive response from the physicists. However, George, the chemist, questioned how they had situated and defined their work, feedback with which Swendsen, Bouzida, and Kumar disagreed, and to which they responded by sharpening and clarifying their own position. Looking at the physicists' responses to these readers' feedback shows how they first needed to comprehend the viewpoints of audiences with different knowledge, experience, criteria, and procedures of understanding before they could begin to revise the DOMC paper.

AUTHORS REVISING TO ADDRESS READER CONCERNS

Much of the feedback from the three scientists who read the DOMC paper helped to clarify what the physicists' audiences, especially those in biology and chemistry, might expect from the paper. Although the physicists were sometimes surprised by this feedback, they generally agreed with it and used it to revise their presentation. This is what they did with David's feedback on a primary data display comparing their simulation results for the DOMC

method with their results for both molecular dynamics and traditional
Monte Carlo (see Fig. 5.1). David responded to this display by questioning
the impression it conveyed. He said that the convergence of the lines for
MD and traditional MC suggested that these methods are actually more efficient than DOMC. As a result of this impression, he wrote, "Not convincing!" at the end of the paragraph in the text that explained the graph. This
paragraph read:

> In Fig. 5.1, we plot the r.m.s displacement obtained for each of the three meth-
> ods. If only the MD and standard MC results are considered, they would seem
> to have converged rapidly to an r.m.s of 0.22Å. However, the DOMC simula-
> tion shows that the real maximum is more than a factor of four higher. The ap-
> parent convergence of MD and standard MC is deceiving, and the true
> relaxation times for these methods are much longer than the simulation time.

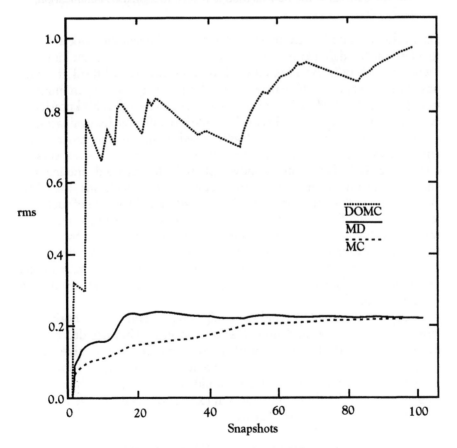

FIG. 5.1.   The physicists' original data display depicting the behavior of MD, MC,
and DOMC.

(Bouzida, Kumar, & Swendsen, draft 15 of the DOMC paper, June 15, 1991, paragraph 41)

Although Swendsen, Kumar, and Bouzida tried to explain this convergence, David relied on the visual presentation and was not convinced by it.

In his response to the physicists, David said that the impression conveyed by the figure potentially rendered their paper uncredible. He explained his concerns in an interview:

> The figure—it didn't make sense. They have established methods, and they agree with each other. The new method doesn't agree. It's way out in left field. Why are you going to believe it? Where's the proof? The authors state that the errors are negligible, but with no proof.... Dead. They have to show that the old methods eventually converge to the new one if you run it long enough. What the data say is the new method is wrong. (personal communication, June 7, 1991)

David also indicated in strong terms that he would reject the work if he was to referee it: "If I didn't know Swendsen and have some respect for his work, I wouldn't accept it. As a ref, I'd read this and trash it.... I think it would have been a very uncredible paper. It's a blind spot" (personal communication, June 7, 1991). His comments, however, suggested that his knowledge of Swendsen, and respect for his work, would have affected his evaluation.

In *A Rhetoric of Science*, Prelli (1989) talked about the acceptance of scientific ideas hinging on the perception that the researcher has respectable qualities (p. 107). He pointed to how past credibility, method, and manner can become important factors in a community's decisions (p. 143). Perelman and Olbrechts-Tyteca (1969) also addressed the role of such factors. They said, "The office of a speaker, no less than his person, forms a context which has an undeniable influence" (p. 319). However, Swendsen, Bouzida, and Kumar would soon be addressing scientists who would not know Swendsen's reputation—especially biologists and chemists who had never heard of Swendsen—and who, as a result, could end up making harsher judgments.

Because they wished to avoid such judgments, the physicists chose to revise their presentation to address David's concerns. They decided to conduct additional, longer simulation runs and to revise their presentation—both text and visuals—to reflect the outcomes of those runs. They hoped that the additional data would do a better job of showing the true behavior of the three methods. An excerpt of the exchange in which they planned these revisions follows:

Swendsen: The important one is he [David] doesn't find it convincing that our method is correct....

Bouzida: Maybe I should show him a longer run?

Swendsen: That's exactly what we need. The plot shows three methods—two old and one new. The two old agree, and we're saying they're wrong because ours is different.... He's reading it as us saying we're right because it's different, but since the others agree it creates the impression that ours is really wrong....

Bouzida: Maybe we should have MD and MC in that graph. I'll do a long run tonight.

Swendsen: We have to say why, and we have to give some run of MC and MD that actually goes up. He said the main reason he believes is because he knows me. His [David's] basic argument is, he said, "Look, MD and MC are methods people reading this are familiar with and believe, and here they give the same answer." Our method gives a different answer so it's wrong. (review meeting for drafts 12, 13, and 14 of the DOMC paper, June 4, 1991)

The physicists also said they needed additional data, and text, to convince audience members who might not share their perspectives: "People reading don't believe simple harmonic oscillator is valid.... It's more convincing if these go up again. Djamal has data, but it's never going to get up that high. We'll have to do it with words. Say that even though the convergence looks terrific, it's wrong. It's wrong because ... " (review meeting for drafts 12, 13, and 14 of the DOMC paper, June 4, 1991).

Swendsen viewed his failure to see these potential problems as an oversight. In an interview in which he reflected on David's feedback, he said,

I didn't realize it. In hindsight I should have realized it. The graph implies something that is not true. We should demonstrate that the methods will eventually all go to the same level. It seemed obvious to me.... I also hadn't realized how short those runs were. And we could easily make long runs to demonstrate, so I was a little upset with myself.... That's one reason you show these things to friends. (personal communication, June 5, 1991)

Swendsen also attributed this oversight to his greater familiarity with the outcomes of the simulations:

I didn't anticipate that objection because I know that if you simulate for a long enough time the MD and MC would come out the same as the DOMC.... Those times would be very long. It's very hard to anticipate objections. People will interpret things in different and peculiar ways. This is actually very straightforward, but not for people not as familiar with the details of the calculation. (personal communication, June 5, 1991)

In the report *On Being a Scientist*, the Committee on the Conduct of Science of the National Academy of Sciences (1989) addressed how people tend to see what they expect to see and fail to notice what they believe should not be there (p. 4). They also, interestingly, talked about how researchers may stop a data run too early because the observations obtained from the run conform to expectations (p. 5).

After the physicists generated the additional data, they added a new display of their data, and they revised the text that explained both the old and the new displays. These displays now showed both shorter and longer runs for each of the three methods (see Figs. 5.2 and 5.3), and the text that explained them distinguished the short-time behavior shown in the one display from the lengthier run shown in the other. This text also explained the simulation method, presented their results, and showed the advantage of their technique in achieving a more rapid convergence to the final value. The expanded section was now three paragraphs long:

> Plots of the *r.m.s* displacements obtained for each of the three methods starting from the same well-equilibrated structure corresponding to the same amount of computer time are shown in Figures 5.2 and 5.3. Figure 5.2 shows the "short-time" behavior of the *r.m.s* fluctuations, while a lengthier run is shown in Figure 5.3. From the short run, the *r.m.s* fluctuations obtained from DOMC exceed the MD fluctuations, and approach the asymptotic value rapidly. (Bouzida, Kumar, & Swendsen, draft 22 of the DOMC paper, August 23, 1991, paragraph 41)

> The plot of the DOMC *r.m.s* fluctuations also shows some kinks (or zigzags). These represent energy-barrier crossings when the molecule changes conformation states. These kinks are also seen in the MD data in Figure 5.3; however, they occur on much longer (and unpredictable) time scales. (Bouzida, Kumar, & Swendsen, draft 22 of the DOMC paper, August 23, 1991, paragraph 42)

> The *r.m.s* fluctuations obtained from MD depend strongly on the initial conditions—both on the initial configuration and the initial random Maxwellian velocities. They don't usually rise as fast as shown in Figure 5.2. Our work indicates that for any initial configuration, the DOMC simulation converges much faster than either standard MC or MD. (Bouzida, Kumar, & Swendsen, draft 22 of the DOMC paper, August 23, 1991, paragraph 43)

As they discussed and worked through these changes, the physicists also began to view them as an opportunity to strengthen their arguments.

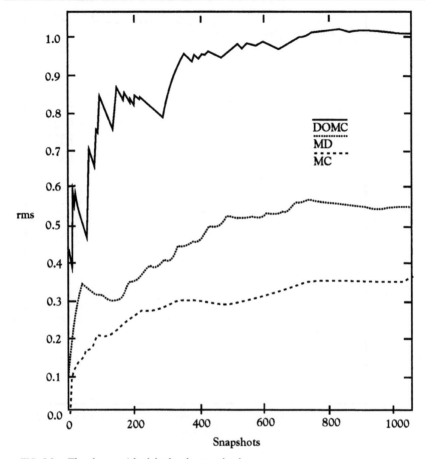

FIG. 5.2.   The physicists' final display showing the shorter run.

Swendsen said, "Something like this is relevant. It's a very strong point in our favor. If we can really pound on this, actually demonstrate that this is wrong and our results are correct, which I think we can" (review meeting for drafts 12, 13, & 14 of the DOMC paper, June 4, 1991). David's feedback thus helped the physicists to revise their presentation to make it clearer and even more persuasive.

AUTHORS REVISING TO CLARIFY DISTINCT POSITIONS

Although Swendsen, Bouzida, and Kumar agreed with David's feedback on their primary data display, they disagreed with George's feedback on two other aspects of their presentation—on how they situated their work in the

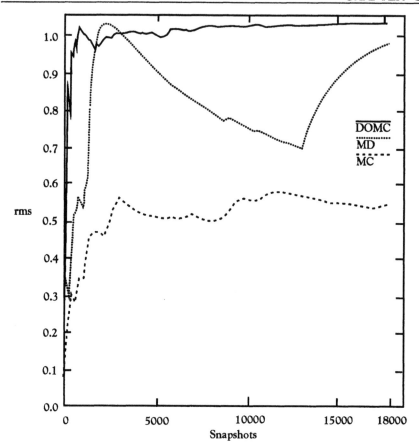

FIG. 5.3. The physicists' final display showing the longer run.

larger field they were addressing and on the objectives they expressed in presenting the work. George conveyed this feedback in an e-mail message to Bouzida, which started out by identifying other work the physicists should have referenced[1]:

> On page 11, the paragraph beginning, "In figure 5 ...," I think you should reference the clear separtation [sic] of time scales associated with dihedral rotations and atomic fluctuations. The mixing of local motions and more global motions tend [sic] to distort the perspective of timescales. Also, these types of MC moves are commonly used, e.g., by Scheraga for his MC and by people like Jeff Scholnick. You should reference these works. (e-mail communication to Djamal Bouzida, June 6, 1991)

George believed the physicists had not sufficiently acknowledged other important work in the field, and he questioned their knowledge of the communities they were addressing: "My general impression is that the article is not written sufficiently cognizant of other work that's in the field, and that it's important for it to be broadened in that sense" (personal communication, June 17, 1991).

George also indicated in his response, like David, that he would have rejected the paper if he had reviewed it:

> If I had reviewed this, it would have been a problem. The review process is very, very, very variable. Some pay less attention to those things. And sometimes it depends on how far out of the field the people are.... If I had gotten it there would have been problems. (personal communication, June 17, 1991)

The physicists, in George's opinion, had not demonstrated adequate knowledge of these communities or of the work being performed in them. They were missing the substantive criterion of expertise: knowledge of alternative methods in the field. George said that this deficiency would pose problems for the physicists when they submitted the work to journals in these fields:

> Another problem is that Bouzida and Swendsen aren't recognized as experts in this line of work. This may cause problems with reviewers who are. Swendsen is known with lattices in the physics community, which is a fairly small focused group of people. Here he's addressing chemists ... and he's saying his is better than anything that's been proposed before. He needs to be able to address what's been proposed before. (personal communication, June 17, 1991)

According to George, Swendsen's reputation in physics was not sufficient for addressing these other communities.

George's concerns with how the physicists had situated their work in the DOMC paper were also related to his sense of its purpose, which he interpreted as being much different from what the physicists had stated. In his e-mail message to Bouzida, he also said:

> A final comment of general nature is related to stating the objective of the methods in the beginning. It seems they are not aimed at carrying out "conventional" MC but instead aimed toward full configurational sampling as might be used in "folding" problems. If this is true, it should be stated and hence the comparison with conventional MD/MC is less valid in proving a point. Instead, a deeper comparison and discussion of methods of Scheraga and Scholnick should be made. (e-mail communication to Djamal Bouzida, June 6, 1991)

When he explained these comments in the interview, George claimed that the objective of the DOMC paper shifted to protein folding while the language did not. Given this shift, he argued, the comparisons between MD and MC, which formed a substantial part of the physicists' text, were less relevant: "Conventional MC and MD are not used for conventional protein folding kinds of problems. They really, I think, should refocus the paper" (personal communication, June 17, 1991). In George's mind, the physicists' extensive comparison of the two methods was inconsistent with their actual purpose. He therefore believed that they needed to revise their presentation to bring it more in line with their objectives.

In explaining this response, George also expressed his sense of the history of the physicists' work. He said:

> I can give my perception of why the paper is written as it is, which determines my reasoning about how it should be altered. The whole thing started two and a half years ago—talking about problems relating to protein folding—the Northrup and McCammon paper. Initially they went after algorithms to improve on sampling for conventional MC. That is sort of this a.r.m, which optimizes the step size in Cartesian space, or at least in the sphere of a given radius. However, my impression is that this convergence characteristic of the smaller curve using the MC/a.r.m wasn't the kind of improvement they hoped for … so they focused on a different aspect of the problem: Can you do something that really folds up and unfolds the molecule? So the shift went to protein folding. (personal communication, June 17, 1991)

George's comments illustrate what Gieryn (1978) referred to as social perceptions of research by peers (p. 107), and what Haas and Flower (1988) referred to when they said:

> The private mental representation that a reader constructs has many facets: it is likely to include a representation of propositional or content information, a representation of the structure—either conventional or unique—of that information, and a representation of how the parts of the text function. In addition, the reader's representation may include beliefs about the subject matter, about the author and his or her credibility, and about the reader's own intentions in writing. (1988, p. 168)

George revealed his beliefs about each of these things and how they fit into a specific organized sense of the field as both intellectual and social constructs.

Swendsen, Bouzida, and Kumar, however, did not see the context that they had constructed for the paper, or the objectives they had specified for it, in the same way George did. Rather than responding in a conciliatory manner, as they had to David's comments, they responded adversarially. They reiterated the fundamental value of the Monte Carlo method and rejected any notion that they were engaging in a loss minimization strategy by shifting the focus of their work. In their discussions with me and with each other—and even in their direct response to George—they openly expressed frustration with his views. Swendsen, for example, said of George's feedback more generally:

> He's reading it from a very different point of view from what it's written as....
> He's just not reading it on the terms it was written.... If that's the criteria for
> accepting or rejecting, which he indicates here it could be for him, then it
> could give trouble that's just not appropriate.... I think there's a lot of misin-
> terpretation here. Some of it may just be George, some of it may be the com-
> munity as a whole. I think part of it is the community. They're just not used to
> doing something this way. (personal communication, July 15, 1991)

These comments also support wider speculations about community effects.

Swendsen also responded to George's comments about his reputation. He said:

> He's classifying us in the line of doing simulations on biological molecules. I'm
> not an expert on that.... So if people are going to look at it on that basis ... I,
> we have addressed what's been proposed before with respect to the problem
> we stated. He's talking about everything that's been proposed before with re-
> spect to biological simulations. He's reading it from a very different point of
> view from what it's written as. On the problem of not being recognized in the
> field—our not being recognized—that's a strange criterion. I guess what I'm
> used to is I present something in a paper, and it's presented on its own
> terms—[I] present an algorithm and expect people to try it regardless of who I
> am. (personal communication, July 15, 1991)

Swendsen asserted that he was well established in the field of condensed matter theoretical physics, and that he was also well known for his work with the Monte Carlo method. At the time of my study, he had published more than 80 papers, and he had been writing on the applications of the Monte Carlo renormalization group for 12 years. He had also been using the Monte Carlo method to conduct simulations for more than 5 years. He said his interest in applying this method to simulations of biological molecules was grounded in his previous inquiries.

Finally, Swendsen also expressed frustration with George's interpretation of their purpose for the paper. He said, "The paper doesn't discuss protein folding [that would be a separate paper]. I guess if you had written a paper on Milton and someone wanted one on Shakespeare, you'd have to completely rewrite the paper" (personal communication, July 15, 1991). He added:

> He doesn't understand what we were doing in our purpose.... My impression
> in reading this is not necessarily that he's hostile, but he's reading it for some-

thing else. He's reading for something and not finding it.... He doesn't seem
to understand.... He seems to think we're only after folding and equilibrium
doesn't matter, and comparison with standard MC and MD doesn't matter.
(personal communication, July 15, 1991)

Swendsen said the difference in perspective in and of itself was not a problem, "The fact he thinks we're doing something other than what we say
we're doing, that's a problem" (personal communication, July 15, 1991).

In addition to expressing frustration with George's feedback to me and to
each other, the physicists also expressed their disagreement with George directly. In his response to George's e-mail message, Bouzida stated explicitly
that the DOMC paper was meant to be similar to Northrup & McCammon's
paper[2]: "The spirit of this paper is similar to Northrup & McCammon's paper
... , where MD, MC and smart MC were compared" (e-mail communication
to George, June 25, 1991). He also addressed George's criticisms of how they
had situated their work. In doing this, he asserted his knowledge of the articles
George had mentioned while also emphasizing how they differed from what
he and his colleagues were trying to do:

> The essence of our methods is to locally optimize both the single atom mo-
> tions and the long-wavelength modes on the fly. I agree that we should refer to
> the works by Scheraga and Go, but not the work by Scholnick. I attended
> Scholnick's talk at the conference. He uses a lattice representation of the pro-
> tein. The bond lengths and bond angles are again kept fixed while the dihed-
> ral angles are allowed to vary. I am not sure I understand his potential energy
> function. It's definitely not the empirical Hamiltonian that most researchers
> use. (e-mail communication to George, June 25, 1991)

Bouzida also cited and addressed specific issues in these articles, which
seemed to lend additional weight to his response: "See for example page
1240 of the article by D. C. Rapaport, H. A. Scheraga macromolecules [sic]
vol. 14, 1981" (e-mail communication to George, June 25, 1991).

These initial verbal responses to George's feedback set the stage for the
physicists' more formal response in their revisions, which shows how disagreements with audience members can lead authors to distinguish and articulate
their own positions even more forcefully. In particular, Swendsen, Bouzida,
and Kumar responded to George's feedback (both that which addressed how
they had situated their work, as well as that which addressed their objectives)
by revising the part of their paper that addressed Northrup and McCammon's
work. They decided to clarify their objectives for the DOMC paper by articu-
lating their concerns with this work even more strongly.

Before addressing the physicists' revisions to this part of the text, it may
be useful to review earlier formulations of this information, along with how

they arrived at these formulations. The physicists had revised this formulation several times before they gave the paper to the three scientists to review. Initially, the paragraph that addressed this work read:

> From experience with the physics of fluids and magnetic systems, we would expect Monte Carlo methods to be preferable for equilibrium properties. However, early work [14] indicated that MD was also more efficient for equilibrium properties, which has led the chemical and biological communities [sic] prefer MD in all cases. This apparent inconsistency stimulated our interest in the search for efficient methods for these problems. (Bouzida, Kumar, & Swendsen, draft 4 of the DOMC paper, April 24, 1991, paragraph 10)

When they reviewed this formulation, Swendsen, Kumar, and Bouzida became sensitive to the fact that their audiences, which had accepted MD as a standard in the field, might find it too critical. Therefore, they decided to tone down the presentation so that it would not offend their readers.[3]

Part of the discussion in which they addressed these concerns follows. Swendsen had boxed and crossed out this paragraph in one of the drafts, and in the review meeting in which they discussed the draft he even addressed the possibility of deleting it:

> Swendsen: I put a question mark by the next paragraph, but I'm not sure why. That paragraph bothers me every time, but I'm not sure why.... I do know some people who would argue with me on expecting Monte Carlo to be preferable for equilibrium properties. There is a small group who claim molecular dynamics is better for equilibrium properties....
>
> Bouzida: What's their argument? Why do they think molecular dynamics is better?
>
> Swendsen: Their argument is.... I don't know. My feeling is to just take it out (review meeting for draft 6 of the DOMC paper, May 9, 1991).

The physicists ended up keeping the paragraph because it contained the only reference to Northrup and McCammon, but they refocused it in order to emphasize their reasons for preferring MC—its flexibility in optimizing efficiency. They also softened their indictment of MD by not expressing as much surprise with biologists' and chemists' acceptance of this method.

The physicists' eventual formulation of this information, which appeared in the draft that the three scientists reviewed, read:

> Early work [18] indicated that MD was more efficient than MC, even for equilibrium properties. However, we have chosen an MC approach because

of the flexibility of the method in optimizing the efficiency. (Bouzida, Kumar, & Swendsen, draft 13 of the DOMC paper, June 3, 1991, paragraph 9)

When he explained the concerns that led up to this version, Bouzida said, "We don't want to say that Monte Carlo is better than molecular dynamics directly. There are cases where MD is better" (personal communication, May 12, 1991). He also said, "The idea was like we were attacking, and that's not true" (personal communication, May 20, 1991). The physicists were thus trying to be sensitive to their readers' perspectives.[4] However, they ended up taking a much different approach when they responded to George.

Because of George's concerns, Swendsen rewrote this formulation yet again. However, instead of toning it down, this time he made the problems and disparities in Northrup and McCammon's work even clearer and less ambiguous. His revision read:

> Early work by Northrup and McCammon [21] indicated that MD was more efficient than MC, even for equilibrium properties. However, this conclusion was based on the incorrect belief that MC required much more computer time to carry out the updating process. When this is corrected, their data on the r.m.s deviations per sweep actually indicates that standard MC is more efficient than MD. We have chosen to base our approach on MC partly for this reason, but primarily because of the flexibility for introducing additional new moves in MC simulations to improve the efficiency. (Bouzida, Kumar, & Swendsen, draft 18 of the DOMC paper, August 16, 1991, sentences 6–9, paragraph 10)

There are several notable changes in this formulation, one of which is the switch from a nonintegral to an integral form of citation (Swales, 1990).[5] Although Swendsen, Bouzida, and Kumar had previously referred to Northrup and McCammon's work using only a number, they now used direct attribution to reference the work. This change enabled the physicists to use these scientists to support their own work: The physicists asserted that these scientists' conclusion actually supported their own conclusions and findings.

When he commented on these changes in a follow-up interview, Bouzida said that Swendsen had requested them because "The way we say it now means we're agreeing with them, and we shouldn't.... Even their data indicate that standard MC is more efficient than standard MD.... So it's going to make the paragraph longer, and better I think, more precise" (personal communication, August 12, 1991). Bouzida had previously articulated quite different concerns; he commented, for example, that "We don't want to say that Monte Carlo is better than molecular dynamics directly. There are cases where MD is better" (personal communication, May 13, 1991). Thus, although the physicists had been concerned with toning down their statements in the earlier drafts, they now wished to make their disagreements and problems with this work more explicit. They articulated their own position more forcefully, and they made the distinctions between their own views and those of their interlocutors even more apparent.

The formulation just shown, however, was not the physicists' final one. After showing another draft of the paper to David and George, they revised it, yet another time, in response to some additional feedback from these scientists.[6] The exchange in which they discussed and negotiated the final revision follows:

Swendsen: George was very concerned about the paragraph on page 3 addressing the work of Northrup & McCammon. His objection—he claimed that Northrup & McCammon say it takes a factor of 10 or longer. George tried to argue they're correct. The big thing he made an issue of is that they probably had paging difficulties because MC required more space. But the whole thing collapses because MD takes more space.

Kumar: He's wrong.... [Proceeds to explain why.]

Swendsen: Well, we're talking about an old Honeywell machine.... Yes, so anyway, I think I talked him out of it. He wants us to modify the paragraph. Let me give you the modification and see what you think.... [Reads modification, which appears later.] ... Okay, so how does that sound? Should I read it again without the introduction?

Kumar: It sounds okay.

Swendsen: [Rereads the modification.] ... I'm not completely satisfied with, "Their observation " because it's an incorrect observation.

Bouzida I like "observation."...

Swendsen: Okay, so we like that. Okay, George will like that. (review meeting for draft 20 of the DOMC paper, August 21, 1991)

The physicists were now concerned with constructing a formulation that satisfied both George and themselves.[7] According to Perelman and Olbrechts-Tyteca (1969), an argument's strength depends on its ability to resist objection (pp. 461–462). It is therefore advisable, they say, for authors to account for everything that is admitted by the audience so as to give the argument its fullest strength (pp. 472–473). That seemed to be a concern for the physicists when they constructed their final formulation. It read:

Early work by Northrup and McCammon [21] indicated that MD was more efficient than MC, even for equilibrium properties. This conclusion was based on their observation [changed from "incorrect belief"] that MC required much more computer time to carry out the updating process. However, the two methods actually require about the same amount of computer time per sweep [added]. When this is corrected for, their data, based on the r.m.s deviations per sweep, [deleted "actually"] indicated that standard MC is more efficient than MD. We have chosen to base our approach on MC partly for this reason, but primarily because of the flexibility for introducing additional new moves in MC simulations to improve the efficiency. (Bouzida, Kumar, & Swendsen, draft 21 of the DOMC paper, August 23, 1991, paragraph 11)

In this final revision, the physicists still addressed the problems with Northrup and McCammon's work, but they tempered their criticisms by removing potentially offensive wording—"incorrect belief" and "actually"—and by adding an explanation to support their claim about the problems with this work—"However, the two methods actually require about the same amount of computer time per sweep."

Finally, George's responses to the physicists' work also raise important issues. They suggest that while authors may endeavor, rhetorically, to have interlocutors adopt certain points of view and roles, they cannot completely control the experiences, viewpoints, and interpretive frameworks audience members bring naturally to any rhetorical situation. In other words, audience members may determine and construct, themselves, the roles they play in a rhetorical situation, even independent of the efforts of the authors. A reader does not have to like or be persuaded by what he or she reads. The text can fail to reach the reader, which seems to be what happened with George.

CONCLUSION

Although studies in the rhetoric of science have tended to focus on the coherent, monovocal endpoint of composing, the findings I present in this and the previous chapter capture the negotiations, uncertainties, disagreements, and messiness that occurred as a result of the physicists' direct interactions with members of their audiences. These things usually disappear in the residual descriptions that scholars, like Knorr-Cetina (1981), say ultimately result when the paper is published (p. 115). What an up-close examination of the physicists' interactions and negotiations with these members of their audiences reveals is a sense of how these personal interests and situational contingencies impacted their composing activities in general, along with how they influenced and shaped their revisions to the DOMC text more particularly. This examination also shows how the DOMC paper took on an active and problematic public life even before it was published.

Finally, my findings in this and the previous chapter move us even further away from traditional conceptions of audience and audience analysis that portray audiences as abstract and static entities and that relegate audience analysis to a single, usually very early stage of the writing process. An alternative is to view audience as a real, physical entity that authors can interact with and come to know (and be influenced by) on a more direct and personal level, as the physicists did with the three scientists. Such processes may be gradual and at times limited, as they were in this case, but they still encourage viewing audiences as dynamic and fluid, as opposed to static entities. In support of such views, every physicist I interviewed during my study emphasized the importance in their work of direct, ongoing interaction with actual audience members. This interaction is science; it is what scientists do. Scientists, like the physicists, rely on such interaction in their everyday work to obtain information about their audiences and to respond to and address their audiences' concerns. How scientists learn to do these things is taken up as the subject of chapter 6.

NOTES

a. Data and figures in this chapter were previously presented in *Technical Communication Quarterly*, 2(1), 1993, Readers and authors: Fictionalized constructs or dynamic collaborations (pp. 22–35), A. M. Blakeslee.

1. George may have addressed his response to Bouzida because he was a member of Bouzida's thesis committee, and he was responding to the thesis at the same time in which he was responding to the DOMC paper.

2. Bouzida, and not Swendsen, responded to George because George had e-mailed his initial reactions directly to Bouzida.

3. The physicists were essentially confronting a community knowledge that contradicted their findings, and they were concerned that those who accepted this knowledge would take offense to this presentation. Miller (1992) addressed this idea of contradicting the weight of scientific commitment in her discussion of how kairos functions in science (p. 320). In order to publish a paper, scientists must present new information that refutes or moves beyond previous claims and ideas. However, they must also acknowledge relevant previous work and situate their own ideas within the context of those existing ideas. This requires diplomacy on the parts of authors so that readers who accept the views being challenged are not alienated.

4. In constructing these early formulations, the physicists exhibited a sensitivity to their readers and to how those readers might perceive and respond to their work. They were concerned with persuading these scientists, and, as a result, they care-

fully considered what information to present and how to array that information to achieve their objectives. Law and Williams (1982) aptly described what the physicists faced and sought to do in this case when they said:

> Structuring a written array in such a way that the paper attracts credibility is thus a delicate balancing act: one needs … to design a context that makes one's own paper important and something that the reader does not wish to put down…. One also needs to mention, structure, and propose a value for, the particulars which form a part of that context in a manner that is recognizably fair and reasonable for the standpoint of the reader. Where the writer succeeds—he is able to guess the relevant concerns and likely interpretive networks of the readers—then the latter will be drawn into the argument. Where he fails, then, of course, the paper fails. (pp. 547–548)

However, in this case George's response suggested that the physicists had failed to guess completely the relevant concerns and interpretive networks of all of their readers. Law and Williams (1982) also addressed the importance of such perceptions, and their relationship to how authors present information:

> The product must be *perceived* by other scientists as having use value. It must be seen as both reliable and relevant. But the perceived reliability and relevance of a product is not something that is independent of the way in which it is presented. Consequently, scientists take great care to present their products to maximum effect. (p. 537)

In a similar vein, Perelman and Olbrechts-Tyteca (1969) said that "Every social circle or milieu is distinguishable in terms of its dominant opinions and unquestioned beliefs … : these views form an integral part of its culture, and an orator wishing to persuade a particular audience must of necessity adapt himself to it" (pp. 20–21).

5. In the previous presentation, the physicists used an impersonal construction (a bracketed 14), rather than a direct attribution, to reference Northrup and McCammon's article. Myers (1989) called such constructions negative politeness strategies. He said criticisms of opposing views are seldom explicit; all criticisms must be posed in acceptable, impersonal, technical terms, or avoided (p. 25). The physicists' impersonal construction also illustrates what Swales (1990) called a nonintegral form of citation. Swales distinguished "integral" and "nonintegral" forms of citation on the basis of whether the researcher's name appears in a statement of attribution or in parentheses, or whether it is referred to numerically, as it was in this case (p. 148).

6. I do not have David's and George's responses to this additional review in my data.

7. I do not have data regarding whether or not George accepted this revised formulation.

6

Learning to Write in Context: Newcomers Getting to Know and Speak to Audiences[a]

Graduate students begin to learn the difficulties of getting to know and speak to their audiences through a mentoring process with their advisors. This socialization process, which occurs slowly and over time, initiates newcomers into a field of cooperative practice. In my study I observed Bouzida being introduced to the complexity of audience issues in the DOMC paper through interactions with Swendsen as Bouzida composed the early drafts of the paper.[1] The whole idea behind having Bouzida write the DOMC drafts, according to Swendsen, was to help him learn how to write a scientific paper. An important part of such activity is learning how to address and adapt one's writing to audiences, which in this case was made more complex by the multidisciplinary audience that was unfamiliar even to Swendsen.

I base my analysis of Swendsen's and Bouzida's mentoring relationship in this chapter on activity theory. A basic tenet of this theory is that students acquire new skills and knowledge by engaging in the activities typically performed in a field under the guidance of more experienced practitioners. Educational researchers Brown, Collins, and Duguid (1989) called such activity- and interaction-based experiences cognitive apprenticeships. Activity, they said, is not separate from or ancillary to learning but rather is integral to it (p. 32). Also integral are the contexts in which newcomers undertake tasks and the guidance and support provided in those contexts: "Students are expected to learn how to solve problems that arise in the context of carrying out complex tasks and to extend and make use of their textbook knowledge by undertaking significant projects guided by an expert in the field" (Collins, Brown, & Newman, 1989, p. 460). Knowledge, according to these scholars, is a product of the activity, context, and culture in which it is developed and used. Activity theory thus attempts to synthesize the social and cognitive components of learning, seeing these as two sides of the same coin instead of as dichotomous or mutually exclusive perspectives (Russell, 1997). In short, such theory recognizes that cognition always takes place as part of a situation and that situations always include people engaging in cognition.

ENCOUNTERING A NEW RHETORICAL SITUATION: BOUZIDA'S APPROACH TO COMPOSING THE INITIAL DOMC DRAFTS

Before working with Swendsen, Bouzida's experience with disciplinary writing tasks outside of his courses was limited to preparing technical progress reports for a previous research project in electrical engineering.[2] He had no experience writing a scientific paper, which was one of the reasons Swendsen asked him to compose the DOMC paper. Comments from other physicists I interviewed in my research suggest that in physics, advanced graduate students are often asked by their advisors to write the initial drafts of journal articles. Each of these physicists said they had engaged in this practice to help their students learn, firsthand, the conventions and purposes of the genre (Bob, Brad, Eric, Lazarus).[3] These physicists also talked about supporting their students' efforts at performing these tasks.

Swendsen once addressed this practice, saying, "It's important for the same reason it's important in English—he's going to have to do it.... Papers are the primary vehicle through which you communicate your work" (personal communication, March 8, 1991). One of the other physicists I interviewed in my research described a process by which graduate students in physics fit themselves into an existing research program under the guidance of their advisors. He said they contribute something original to the research by moving it in new directions, and they write their theses and initial publications based on their work on these projects (Bob, personal communication, May 1, 1991). The process that Bob described is similar to that which Bouzida experienced. Bouzida's thesis and initial publications reported his application of the DOMC simulation method to biological molecules. This work was initiated and directed by Swendsen but carried out primarily by Bouzida. It seemed fitting, therefore, that Bouzida write the papers addressing the work.

When Bouzida composed the initial DOMC draft, he relied extensively on the earlier conference paper that he had written with Swendsen and Kumar. Bouzida essentially added information to this paper based on his sense of what his audiences for it would want and need to know. In an interview after he composed the draft, Bouzida said that the scientists in his audiences—biologists and chemists in particular—knew very little about Dynamically Optimized Monte Carlo and therefore needed detailed explanations of the method (personal communication, March 7, 1991).

Because of this concern with explaining their methods to biologists and chemists, Bouzida included two sections on methods in his initial draft. These sections, titled "Description of the Method" and "Efficiency of Simulation Methods," contained several mathematical equations showing how the DOMC method calculates the properties of biological systems (see Appendix A for an excerpt from the first of these sections). They also contained detailed descriptions of the standard Monte Carlo method from which the DOMC method was derived, and of molecular dynamics. Finally, Bouzida also described how the physicists had used the DOMC method to simulate various types of molecules. He addressed their application of the method to fairly complicated, three-dimensional systems and then to a simpler, one-dimensional system. When he described the information he included in these sections, and in the draft in general, he said:

> One thing that we had to do was first describe the importance of simulating molecules—why is it important? The second thing is to talk about what questions are important when you simulate molecules. Next are the methods. Here I have to discuss everything.... When I described the method I went directly to the general formulation, which is like three-dimensional equations. (Bouzida, personal communication, March 7, 1991)

He also said that he based his decisions about how to arrange the information in these sections (e.g., his decision to present the three-dimensional systems before presenting the one-dimensional system) on his sense of what his audiences would expect from the paper (personal communication, March 7, 1991).

The three remaining parts of the initial draft were the introduction, discussion, and conclusion. Bouzida copied most of the introduction from the conference paper.[4] The two other sections in the initial draft—the discussion and conclusion—were incomplete. Bouzida left the conclusion blank and then wrote one paragraph for the discussion. He concluded this section with an ellipsis to signal that it needed further development. He also said in an interview that he hoped Swendsen and Kumar would write the discussion section because, as coauthors, they should contribute something to the paper: "I hope Swendsen and Kumar write the discussion. I can't write everything. Their names are on it too.... I'm going to write some of this, but there might be things they want to say" (personal communication, March 7, 1991). It may be no accident that Bouzida shied away from these two sections of the paper since they typically contain more elaborations of the paper's arguments and contributions than the other sections of a journal article.

Bouzida's inclusion of so much detail in the initial DOMC draft may have reflected his greater familiarity with the technical aspects of his work than with the rhetorical skills he needed to present that work persuasively to other scientists. Although he chronicled many aspects of the research the physicists had done, he did not position that research as part of an argument about the field's knowledge of simulations, which is not unlike the approach he took with the two conference presentations he gave (see chap. 3). Nor did he select and frame the methods in ways that would be most useful to biologists and chemists.

Bouzida's approach to composing this initial draft also seemed to reflect his greater familiarity with documents, such as the progress reports he had written for his previous advisor, that also emphasize detailed explanations of technical procedures over arguments about research methods and findings. Swendsen once said that such responses are common among graduate students because students learn the technical aspects of their work before they learn the rhetorical strategies they need to present that work to their audiences (personal communication, March 8, 1991). Students usually write most easily, he said, about those aspects of their work on which they have spent most of their time. He also explained that some of this information may be of little or no interest to the readers of journal articles, which was one of the concerns he expressed when he responded to the initial DOMC draft. Thus, Bouzida, lacking support and guidance as he initially undertook this unfamiliar composing task, not surprisingly, relied on previous experiences and strategies. His efforts and difficulties with the task—especially with constructing and arranging a presentation that would persuade their audiences—became focal points for Swendsen's response to this draft.

IMPARTING AUDIENCE KNOWLEDGE THROUGH RESPONSE: SWENDSEN'S FEEDBACK

Swendsen offered Bouzida both oral and written feedback on all of the drafts he produced.[5] After Bouzida completed each draft, he gave it to Swendsen to review. Swendsen then wrote comments on the draft, sometimes inserting separate pages to elaborate or add information. Swendsen returned the drafts to Bouzida when the three physicists met to review them, which was usually 2 or 3 days after Bouzida had produced and submitted a draft for review. During these meetings, Swendsen explained his written comments and told Bouzida what to do to improve the draft. Bouzida usually took notes on Swendsen's concerns during these meetings and asked Swendsen to clarify those concerns that he did not understand. This general pattern was repeated for all of the 22 drafts Bouzida composed. In this chapter, I focus only on the first few drafts.

When Swendsen reviewed and wrote comments on the initial DOMC draft, he displayed his knowledge of their audiences for this work and of what they would need to do to persuade those audiences. He focused on two aspects of Bouzida's presentation: the way in which he had structured the information in the draft and the amount of technical detail he had included, especially in the two methods sections. Swendsen seemed especially concerned with the information that addressed the application of the physicists' method to one- and three-dimensional systems. In the part of the text that addressed this information, next to paragraph 11 (see Appendix A), he wrote "1D first" and "first solve the problem for an SHO." When he discussed these concerns in the review meeting, Swendsen told Bouzida that their audiences would find the current arrangement confusing because it presented more difficult information first:

> That needs to be put first. We need to present an argument that somebody not really familiar with Monte Carlo can understand ... so they can get the idea. They can then see the similarity, the resemblance [between the uses of Monte Carlo and molecular dynamics]. Next say, "We're going to first do this with a simple harmonic oscillator." Get at strategy. What are we trying to do? We're going to develop a method for a simple harmonic oscillator with an unknown coupling constant.... Do that first. (review meeting for draft 1 of the DOMC paper, March 5, 1991)

Swendsen held a different perspective than Bouzida on how their audiences would read and interpret this information and on how, therefore, the physicists should present it.

In his response to this initial draft, Swendsen also told Bouzida that he should work on constructing a more succinct, tightly focused, and persuasive argument:

> We don't want to make a presentation here to somebody who knows how the method works.... We're making an argument to people who don't know how the method works and who don't necessarily want to use it or want to read this.... What we have to do is we have to explain the logic of our thinking.... We need the sections broken up so people can follow it and a very hard hitting abstract and introduction. (review meeting for draft 1 of the DOMC paper, March 5, 1991)

Swendsen based these suggestions, once again, on his perception of their audiences, especially biologists and chemists, who might not even want to read the paper.

Although biologists' and chemists' lack of familiarity with the DOMC method was an important consideration for both physicists as they composed the DOMC paper, Swendsen's response made it apparent that he and

Bouzida took very different approaches to addressing it. These approaches may have reflected their respective levels of expertise with addressing audiences. For example, although Bouzida was concerned with explaining the physicists' work in great detail so that biologists and chemists would understand it better, Swendsen was concerned with positioning the work as part of an argument about their simulation methods. Biologists and chemists, he said, would find little reason to read the paper or even to understand the methods unless they were persuaded to do so. Swendsen summarized these concerns in an interview after the first review meeting:

> What I was most concerned with today was the structure of the paper so people could read the paper and see what was valuable in it.... We need to present an argument that somebody not really familiar with Monte Carlo can understand, so they can get the idea.... I by no means gave him a neat prescription. (personal communication, March 8, 1991)

Swendsen's final comment here also sheds light on the manner in which he typically responded to Bouzida. Swendsen's written comments on Bouzida's drafts were usually suggestive and unelaborated (e.g., he would write names to indicate a need for citations, phrases or abbreviations to indicate information he wanted Bouzida to include, and brackets to signal a need for moving or elaborating information). He seldom gave Bouzida fully explicit instructions for addressing his concerns in the revisions.[6] In fact, without the elaboration that Swendsen usually provided in the review meetings, Bouzida had difficulty in addressing Swendsen's written concerns. Even with the elaboration, Bouzida often had difficulties understanding what Swendsen wanted him to do in the drafts and making the revisions he requested. Swendsen's incompleteness, however, was deliberate. He responded in this manner, he said, so that Bouzida could gain experience addressing and responding to the problems in the text on his own (personal communication, May 21, 1991).

Bouzida, however, was unaware of Swendsen's intentions to teach him rhetorical skills.[7] He viewed his responsibilities in composing and revising the drafts of the DOMC paper as natural outcomes of his collaboration with Swendsen. He believed that it was logical for him to help Swendsen in this regard because the two of them had worked together on the project. Furthermore, their dynamic during this part of the project was similar to their previous dynamic, in which Bouzida conducted simulations and performed much of the technical work on the project while Swendsen commented on and directed his efforts. Bouzida perceived Swendsen's feedback, therefore, not as professional or rhetorical instruction per se but as input from someone who was more experienced than he was and who better understood the requirements of the task.

ADDRESSING A MENTOR'S FEEDBACK:
BOUZIDA'S RESPONSE TO SWENDSEN'S CONCERNS
WITH THE DOMC DRAFTS

The incomplete nature of Swendsen's feedback seemed to pose problems for Bouzida when he tried to respond to that feedback.[8] He continued to have difficulties determining what information to include in the paper and how to effectively arrange and present the information.[9] Bouzida even acknowledged these difficulties in my interview with him after the initial review meeting:

> Swendsen says I need lots of work in here. There are lots of things I discuss in one subsection, but I need to rearrange things. The problem is that this paper has everything, but I need to rearrange things.... In other words, I have to expand the introduction and explain all these things. There are a lot of things that I've put in other subsections that I can condense and put in the introduction.... One thing is how to get this order, get these sections. You have to have this flow. It's like you have all these pieces and you need to glue them together. You need the order. That's what I'm having trouble with at this point. (personal communication, March 7, 1991)

Bouzida also commented on Swendsen's concerns with the technical detail in this draft and on his concerns with presenting information in it that would be appropriate for the members of their audiences:

> The other thing is results. We have a lot of results, so it's a question of which ones we want to show.... When I say what kind of results, I mean what kind of figures—like all these tables I have to get rid of. Now I have to decide what to put instead. I'll base my decision on results on which ones actually show that one method is better than another—I think. The other thing is what parameters people [biologists and chemists] are interested in. I'm a physicist, so I don't know. It depends on the journal. So this part, it might change—it depends on. (personal communication, March 7, 1991)

Bouzida's comments about basing his decision of what results to include on which of those results demonstrate the superiority of their methods seem to suggest a concern with constructing an argument that his audiences would find persuasive. However, his qualification, "I think," and the other concerns he raises in this excerpt also exhibit his uncertainties about how to accomplish that.

In revising the initial DOMC draft, Bouzida tried to address Swendsen's concerns. He combined the two methods sections, and he moved the information about the one-dimensional system before the information on the three-dimensional systems. Despite these changes, however, Swendsen still expressed concerns with the amount of detail in the text, which was something Bouzida did not address in the revision, and with the organization of the information. Swendsen focused most of his attention, as he had previously, on the section of the paper that addressed the application of their method to three-dimensional systems. Although Bouzida had moved this section further back in the text, it was still positioned prominently in the paper. Bouzida had also failed to eliminate the detail from this section that Swendsen had said was unnecessary. In response to this detail, Swendsen recommended subordinating the section—especially the equations it contained—to an appendix. The exchange in which they discussed this change follows:

> Swendsen: I'm not sure where the three-dimensional method should go. We might put it in an appendix.
>
> Bouzida: I think it's very important.
>
> Swendsen: It's extremely important, but it interrupts the logic of the paper.
>
> Bouzida: Appendix?
>
> Swendsen: You don't like that idea?
>
> Bouzida: No. [Bouzida explained that the equations express information not conveyed by the one-dimensional system.]
>
> Swendsen: I agree, but I'm talking about the equations and the derivations of the forms, which get a bit technical. We should definitely say that in the paper, but.... That's algebra. [Swendsen again articulates a concern with the amount of detail in the text.]
>
> Bouzida: I think we should say that....
>
> Swendsen: It's a matter of the logic of the paper and how it reads.
>
> Bouzida: Those [other] equations—I think those should go out....
>
> Swendsen: You don't have to do the algebra for people, so that can go here....
>
> Bouzida: One can write this and put that in the appendix.
>
> Swendsen: No, you don't put [information that is important to the argument].... You put things [in the appendix] that people don't need; for example, the algebra ....
>
> Bouzida: So are we just going to talk about 3-D in an appendix?
>
> Swendsen: Just the equations. [Swendsen explained again what to put in the appendix and why.] (review meeting for draft 2 of the DOMC paper, March 8, 1991)

Swendsen emphasized in this exchange, just as he did in his response to the initial draft, the need to structure the information more logically and to present in the paper only that information that their audience members would find useful. Bouzida, on the other hand, exerting more authority than he had previously, argued that the information in this section is, in fact, of interest to their audiences and should remain in the primary text. Bouzida's reluctance to make the revision, and his concern with subordinating the information, were also evident later in the meeting when he questioned what would be left of the section:

Swendsen: Okay, the problem is right here in the methods section, and the problem is to get the logic of the development....

Bouzida: Okay, you said all this goes in the appendix?

Swendsen: Yes, and you refer to the appendix for an explanation of how the equations are derived. [Swendsen explained to Bouzida, yet again, what information needed to be placed in the appendix and the reasons for subordinating this information.]

Bouzida: So, it's going to be like two small paragraphs then? (review meeting for draft 2 of the DOMC paper, March 8, 1991)

Bouzida expresses his dismay here that only two short paragraphs from the original section would remain in the body of the text. As a newcomer to the discipline, Bouzida conceivably had difficulty accepting that some information, which was interesting and novel to him, might not be interesting or novel to the members of his audience. He thus continued to have trouble discerning the amounts and kinds of information that members of his audience would find interesting.

ESTABLISHING A FOCUS: SWENDSEN'S REVISIONS

Eventually, Swendsen became frustrated with Bouzida's difficulties with understanding and applying his feedback. As a result of this frustration, Swendsen undertook his own revisions to the text without any input from Bouzida. He did this after Bouzida had produced three drafts of the DOMC paper. When he explained these actions to me in an interview, Swendsen said that he was frustrated that the problems with the drafts were not being resolved more quickly (personal communication, May 21, 1991). He also acknowledged his continued concern with allowing Bouzida to engage in the task independently so that he would learn how to do it:

I'm trying to get Bouzida to do as much as possible, or I probably would have done that sooner.... I did it because I felt it was necessary right there. And I think it would have taken longer if I hadn't. Writing a paper with multiple authors generally does take longer. Bouzida is still having trouble looking at the whole paper. I guess that wasn't happening. It takes time. Here the things he was worried about in this last draft were totally inappropriate. (personal communication, May 21, 1991)

Swendsen explained to me that he revised the DOMC draft at this stage both to establish a stronger focus for the paper, one that would make more sense to their audiences, and to redirect the revision process: "The thing I was concerned with was the order of and structure of the argument and how it proceeded.... I was basically trying to pull out and clarify or elaborate ideas in parts" (personal communication, May 21, 1991). (See Appendix B for excerpts from Swendsen's revision.)

When Bouzida saw the outcome of Swendsen's actions, his response was somewhat mixed. On one hand Bouzida expressed his relief that Swendsen was finally giving him more direct and explicit feedback. He had been asking Swendsen all along for such feedback. He also seemed satisfied with the outcome of Swendsen's actions, especially in regard to the paper's structure. He told me, "I think we have the structure of the paper completely, and that's important" (personal communication, May 3, 1991). In fact, the structure Swendsen established for the paper in this draft remained intact, for the most part, throughout the rest of the composing process.

On the other hand, Bouzida also expressed concern with the extent to which Swendsen had shortened the paper—Swendsen was concerned with eliminating detail that he thought their readers would find unnecessary. Bouzida also expressed concern that Swendsen seemed to disregard mechanical problems. The latter actually bothered Bouzida throughout the drafting process. He tended, with all of the drafts, to be much more concerned than Swendsen with the length of the text, its physical attributes (e.g., headings and subheadings), style, and mechanical correctness. He was concerned with and tended to get bogged down in producing polished, finished-looking texts. The initial DOMC draft, for example, superficially resembled a polished, final paper—it had a title, abstract, and finished-looking results section, in addition to the introduction and the two methods sections. Bouzida even admitted that these concerns made him reluctant to make substantive changes in the text; he said he feared that such changes would disrupt its flow and appearance (personal communication, March 18, 1991). Swendsen, on the other hand, was concerned almost exclusively with making substantive changes.

These differences in the two physicists' rhetorical concerns were often evident in their exchanges during the review meetings. Swendsen focused in the meetings primarily on conceptual and structural concerns, whereas

Bouzida frequently tried to redirect his attention to local, stylistic concerns, as illustrated in this exchange:

Bouzida: I don't know, I think I created too many subtitles.

Swendsen: They're easy to get rid of. On the methods ... it is common-place to carry out ... something about preliminary calcula-tions. Maybe set that off a bit clearer....

Bouzida: You're saying that goes first and without the subtitle?

Swendsen: No, I'm sorry. We should have it in. We should have it in explicitly because this audience isn't going to be familiar with it.... Put in the r.m.s and say what the tau and the ab-solute value are.... And then you want to talk about....

Bouzida: Is it going to be like a subsection?

Swendsen: I don't care if they're [the subtitles] there or not. Actually, they're good. Put them in as much as possible. I like the subsection titles.... Way back in the beginning we say the philosophy is you develop a .... (review meeting for draft 2 of the DOMC paper, March 8, 1991)

Although Swendsen addresses Bouzida's concerns with subtitles in this in-teraction, he also steers the discussion back toward the content of the draft. Swendsen's general lack of attention to such local issues often frustrated Bouzida.

In large part, Swendsen's and Bouzida's differing concerns in composing the DOMC paper seemed to be related to their different approaches to composing more generally. Swendsen's approach to composing was guided by concerns with setting goals, which typically were related to persuading his audiences, and with making plans to achieve those goals. Throughout the DOMC project, Swendsen exhibited a continued sensitivity both to his audiences and to his purposes for writing. He once described his ap-proach by saying:

When I understand something I always write it down neatly.... So I have a lot of these things written or at least an idea of the arguments when I write.... I write the pieces and fit them together. I don't worry about phrasings, details, transitions.... I don't worry about how A flows into B— you might have B before A in the final version.... I guess the order with which you attack things might be personal preference. I don't know anybody who starts at the beginning, writes the abstract and introduction. I think al-most everyone has a highly recursive process. (personal communication, March 8, 1991)

Swendsen's decisions about what information to present and how to present that information seemed to be based on his evolving sense of purpose and audience as the research and the composing processes unfolded—Bereiter and Scardamalia's "two-way interaction between continuously developing knowledge and a continuously developing text" (1987, p. 12).

In contrast to Swendsen's recursive and generative composing process, Bouzida's process seemed to be grounded in much different concerns, with an emphasis on the content generation and writing that seemed to be more characteristic of Bereiter and Scardamalia's (1987) knowledge-telling approach. Bouzida once told me:

> One thing that's very important when you write is outlining. You need an outline.... There's a method called divide and conquer. You want to make your problem a sequence of problems and work on each one separately.... That's why in papers you have sections and subsections. You just concentrate on particular ones then.... I find that much easier. I think everyone does that.... Like with this draft I just concentrated on the methods and I didn't touch the applications section. (personal communication, March 18, 1991)

Although Swendsen tended to be sensitive to the contingencies inherent in all textual production, Bouzida seemed much more concerned throughout the process with making the writing precise and predictable. These different concerns with and approaches to composing influenced Swendsen's and Bouzida's interactions—and the outcomes of those interactions—throughout their work on the DOMC paper.

CONCLUSION

My findings in this chapter (in conjunction with those in chap. 3) suggest that the process of acquiring rhetorical knowledge in a domain, particularly knowledge of how to address one's audiences, is a long, slow one that grows from interaction and engagement in domain-specific activities. Bouzida's experiences composing the initial DOMC drafts, and Swendsen's efforts to support those experiences, show this process, along with some of the difficulties that at times may inhibit it. Although Swendsen supported Bouzida's efforts at composing all 22 of the DOMC drafts, the suggestive and unelaborated nature of Swendsen's feedback occasionally posed difficulties for Bouzida, who was writing a scientific journal article for the first time and who was also learning about and struggling to effectively address his audiences, both in his own community and in the communities of biology and chemistry.

My examination of these difficulties, and of Bouzida's experiences with this process more generally, suggests that direct involvement in the activities of a domain, accompanied by the support of a mentor or more experienced practitioner, provides important experience that moves students into fuller participation in the domain. In her study of an undergraduate biology student, Haas (1994) also found that her subject, Eliza, learned about the rhetorical uses of language in science while working in a laboratory setting with a mentor. Haas's findings, as do mine, reconfirm Brown, Collins, and Duguid's (1989) argument that education entails becoming an insider through situated experience that supports learning.

Appendix A

Excerpts From The First Methods Section ("Description Of The Method") In Bouzida's Initial Domc Draft

Paragraph 9: Common Procedures for Performing MC Calculations

In this paragraph, which begins the first methods section he presents, Bouzida addresses common procedures for conducting MC calculations but notes an exception in regard to biological systems. He positions DOMC as the solution to this exception.

> It has been common practice to do MC calculations by performing two consecutive sets of simulations. From the first set, optimized values of the relevant parameters are obtained. These values are then used in a second set of longer simulations to compute the different physical quantities of interest. Because the parameters are optimized globally from the first set of simulations, a certain homogeneity of the system is assumed. Unfortunately, this assumption does not hold for biological systems. A local optimization is then needed when simulating such systems. In our new methods, which we denote Dynamically Optimized Monte Carlo (DOMC), step sizes are optimized locally as the simulation progresses. (Bouzida, Kumar, & Swendsen, draft 1 of the DOMC paper, March 5, 1991, paragraph 9)

Paragraph 10: Additional Characteristics of Biological Systems

In this paragraph, Bouzida addresses another characteristic of biological systems and how MC accounts for it.

Another characteristic of biological systems is the highly anisotropic time-dependent nature of the interatomic forces. As a result, atomic motions are opposed by hard forces in certain directions whereas motions in other directions are opposed by softer ones. In our method, both the anisotropy and inhomogeneity are taken into account resulting in strongly biased MC trial moves in the easy directions. (Bouzida, Kumar, & Swendsen, draft 1 of the DOMC paper, March 5, 1991, paragraph 10)

Paragraph 11: Ellipsoids

In this paragraph, Bouzida explains how, to account for the anisotropy, moves are sampled from an ellipsoid rather than the usual sphere. This paragraph begins a very technical explication and derivation of several equations, and is the one Swendsen flagged with his comments "1D first" and "first solve the problem for an SHO" when he reviewed the draft.

To account for the local anisotropy of the environment of each atom, these moves are sampled from an ellipsoid, rather than the more usual sphere. The ellipsoids surrounding atoms are of different sizes to account for the inhomogeneity of the molecule. Moves in an ellipsoid are generated by the transformation matrix D_{ij}, so that the trial move d_i is generated by

$$d_i = \sum_{i=1}^{3} D_{ij} v_j, i = 1,2,3 \tag{2}$$

where v_j is a random vector chosen from a unit sphere. Our objective is to optimize the value of the step d_i in the ellipsoid. (Bouzida, Kumar, & Swendsen, draft 1 of the DOMC paper, March 5, 1991, paragraph 11)

Paragraph 12: Derivations of Equations

In this paragraph, Bouzida continues to work through and show how he derived the various equations. This paragraph contains the information that Swendsen eventually relegated to an appendix.

To calculate D_{ij}, we consider a simple anisotropic model of the form

$$H = \frac{1}{2} \sum_{ij} k_{ij} x_i x_j \tag{3}$$

where k_{ij} is a real symmetric matrix of string constants. To simplify the notation, Let [sic] $K_{ij} = \frac{1}{2}\beta k_{ij}$. We can easily show that K_{ij} can be found from the simulation by solving the linear system of equations

$$[\beta \Delta E d_l d_m] = \sum_{ij} K_{ij}[d_i d_j d_l d_m]l, m = 1,2,3 \qquad (4)$$

where ΔE denotes the change of energy for an attempted move d_i and the square brackets indicate an average over all attempted moves, whether or not they were accepted. In matrix notation, the scaling relation for this problem is written as

$$D^t \cdot K \cdot D = F^2 \qquad (5)$$

where D^t is the transpose of the transformation matrix D, and F is a scale factor that is chosen to optimize the efficiency of the simulation as discussed below. From equation (5), we can deduce that D is proportional to a unitary matrix that diagonalizes the matrix K which is obviously the matrix formed by the eigenvectors of K. The transformation matrix D is then given by

$$D_{in} = F(\lambda_n) - \frac{1}{2}V_{in} \qquad (6)$$

where λ_n is an eigenvalue of K_{ij} and V_{in} is the corresponding normalized eigenvector. The solution then entails the construction of the matrix K_{ij} from equation 4, and its diagonalization. This procedure is done and repeated every MC cycle, and D_{ij} is updated to adapt to the changing local environment of each atom. (Bouzida, Kumar, & Swendsen, draft 1 of the DOMC paper, March 5, 1991, paragraph 12)

Paragraph 13: Broader Application of the Method

In this paragraph, Bouzida describes other applications of their method.

So far, we have described motions in which only single atoms are involved. These moves permit a very good local relaxation of the system. However, large-scale motions involving many groups of atoms are needed in order to achieve a global relaxation. Our method is not restricted to single atom moves. It can also be applied to more general moves such as global rotations of a group of atoms around specified flexible bonds. A representation of the coordinate transformation is obtained in terms of the parameters of the rotation—the angle of rotation.... [continues explaining how this works].

(Bouzida, Kumar, & Swendsen, draft 1 of the DOMC paper, March 5, 1991, paragraph 13)

Paragraph 14: Achieving Even Greater Efficiency

In this paragraph, Bouzida describes a situation in which the method is even more efficient.

> This method is especially efficient when the rotations considered are correlated. Groups of two or three angles can be formed. Random angle jumps will then be generated from ellipsoids as described above. The new maximum angle jumps will be dependent on each other and the straight averages obtained when performing the global rotations. (Bouzida, Kumar, & Swendsen, draft 1 of the DOMC paper, March 5, 1991, paragraph 14)

Paragraph 18: Set Up for Discussion of Standard MC

In this paragraph, Bouzida defines the parameters for the application of standard MC and DOMC. I include this paragraph because it corresponds to parts of the excerpt from the revisions Swendsen made, which I include in Appendix B.

> In the following subsections, we will apply the standard Metropolis Monte Carlo, the molecular dynamics, and the DOMC methods to a simple harmonic oscillator in order to test their efficiency. The scaling relation for this system is

$$\frac{1}{2}k\beta\Delta^2 = F^2, \beta = \frac{1}{k_B T} \tag{8}$$

> where k is the spring constant, Δ is the maximum step size used in the simulation. For $V(x) = x^2$ with $\beta = 1$, this equation reduces to

$$\Delta^2 = F^2 \tag{9}$$

> The constant F is a scale factor that is chosen to optimize the different parameters of the simulation. These parameters are the average acceptance ratio $\langle P \rangle$, the autocorrelation time τ, and both r.m.s and absolute displacements per MC-step defined as $\sqrt{\langle d^2 \rangle}$ and $\langle |d| \rangle$, where d represents a trial move between $[-\Delta, \Delta]$ and the angle brackets indicate the thermal average. These parameters vary as a function of the maximum step size Δ. (Bouzida, Kumar, & Swendsen, draft 1 of the DOMC paper, March 5, 1991, paragraph 18)

Appendix B

Excerpts From Swendsen's Revision Of The DOMC Draft

Paragraph 15: Forecasting

In this paragraph, which was added, Swendsen sets up the revised method section that follows and establishes the scope of what he and his coauthors do in the paper. He also alludes to subsequent papers, which is where he now says they will address the larger systems.

> In this paper we present a description of our basic approach and illustrate its advantages by applying it to a small molecule, adenosine. The efficient application of this approach to larger molecules is greatly [sic] by including optimized large-scale moves that will be described in a subsequent paper. (Bouzida, Kumar, & Swendsen, draft 4 of the DOMC paper, April 24, 1991, paragraph 15)

Paragraph 16: DOMC—1-d SHO

In this paragraph, Swendsen sets up and forecasts the revised methods section, which now begins with a discussion of the application of the method to the simpler, one-dimensional systems. He relegated the discussion of the three-dimensional system, which Bouzida had originally placed first in the section, to an appendix.

> In developing the DOMC approach, we began with an analysis of an MC simulation of a one-dimensional simple harmonic oscillator (SHO). The equations we developed turned out to be very robust when applied to more general problems. for [sic] reasons we explain below. In this section, we will first discuss the $d = 1$ SHO, while leaving the details of the $d = 3$ anisotropic SHO for an appendix. We will then discuss applications of DOMC to anharmonic systems. (Bouzida, Kumar, & Swendsen, draft 4 of the DOMC paper, April 24, 1991, paragraph 16)

Paragraphs 17–20: DOMC Applied to $d = 1$ SHO, Acceptance Ratio, MC Studies of $d = 1$ SHO, RMS and Absolute Displacement

In this series of paragraphs, Swendsen begins his explication of the d = 1 SHO by addressing the parameters of the simulations. However, rather than just defining and describing them, as Bouzida had (see paragraph 18 in Appendix A), he presents them more in terms of an argument by developing them and focusing on the significance of the information. For example, he emphasizes the efficiency of an MC simulation and what that efficiency is determined by and depends on. Where Bouzida says "finally, the r.m.s and absolute displacements are also important quantities" (draft 1 of the DOMC paper, March 5, 1991, paragraph 23), Swendsen says, "The simplest measures of efficiency are the r.m.s and average absolute displacements," followed by an explication of why this is so (draft 4 of the DOMC paper, April 24, 1991, paragraph 20).

The potential energy of a $d = 1$ SHO is given by $V(x) = \frac{1}{2}kx^2$. The efficiency of an MC simulation is determined by the choice of maximum step size Δ, which depends on both the coupling constant k and the temperature through the scaling relation

$$\frac{1}{2}K\beta\Delta^2 = F^2 \tag{1}$$

where $\beta = \dfrac{1}{k_B T}$. If we can determine the optimal scale factor F for any SHO, we have solved the problem for all such models. (Bouzida, Kumar, & Swendsen, draft 4 of the DOMC paper, April 24, 1991, paragraph 17)

An important quantity for understanding the efficiency of MC simulations is the average acceptance ratio $\langle P \rangle$, which is defined as the ratio of accepted moves to trial moves during a simulation. The acceptance ratio decreases monotonically (and approximately exponentially) as a function of step size Δ. This occurs because small trial step sizes produce correspondingly small energy changes and high acceptance ratios, while large moves have a high probability of being rejected due to a large energy increase. In both extremes, the sampling is expected to be inefficient. (Bouzida, Kumar, & Swendsen, draft 4 of the DOMC paper, April 24, 1991, paragraph 18)

To judge the efficiency for a given value of Δ, we have performed a series of MC studies of a $d = 1$ SHO, $V(x) = x^2$ with $\beta = 1$. These choices are convenient because the optimal value of Δ for these parameters is identical to the optimal value of F. Δ was varied from 0.5 to 5.0 in steps of 0.5, and each data point used a run of 10,000 MC-steps. We monitored the autocorrelation time τ, and two measures of the displacements per MC-step: $\sqrt{\langle d^2 \rangle}$ and $\langle |d| \rangle$, where d represents the displacement during an MC move and the angular brackets indicate the usual thermal average. (Bouzida, Kumar, & Swendsen, draft 4 of the DOMC paper, April 24, 1991, paragraph 19)

The simplest measures of efficiency are the *r.m.s* and average absolute displacements, since we would expect that larger steps correspond to moving more rapidly through phase space. These quantities should go to zero for small *Delta* since each trial move is small. At the other extreme, for very large Δ, most of the moves are rejected because they involve the large energy changes, and the average displacement is again small. We therefore expect the maxima which are seen in the graphs for these quantities in figures ?? and ??. The maximum *r.m.s* displacement $\sqrt{\langle d^2 \rangle}$ occurs at $\Delta = 2.62$, while $\langle |d| \rangle$ has a maximum at the slightly smaller value of $\Delta = 1.75$. The optimum choice of Δ clearly depends on precisely what is being optimized, but it is also important to note that the maxima are rather broad in both cases. (Bouzida, Kumar, & Swendsen, draft 4 of the DOMC paper, April 24, 1991, paragraph 20)

NOTES

[a]Data from this chapter appeared in *Journal of Business and Technical Communication, 11*(2), 125–169. Copyright © 1997, by A. M. Blakeslee. Reprinted by permission of Sage Publications, Inc.

1. The exchanges I examine in this chapter illustrate the manner in which Swendsen typically responded to Bouzida and the processes of feedback and response that surrounded and shaped the initial drafts of the DOMC paper. During these early stages of the process, Bouzida experienced the most difficulties understanding and addressing his audiences, and understanding the new and unfamiliar requirements of scientific journal articles.

2. Before working with Swendsen, Bouzida had worked with another advisor in electrical engineering. He left this project after 3 years when his fellowship funding ran out.

3. The practices of these physicists in regard to teaching the rhetorical conventions of scientific papers also seem to be consistent with recent theories of genre. According to these theories, genres are marked less by recurring organizational patterns than by recurring purposes, such as the construction and dissemination of knowledge (Bazerman, 1994, pp. 79, 82, 99–100; Berkenkotter & Huckin, 1995, pp. 2–25; Miller, 1984, pp. 151, 155, 157–159, 163, 165; Schryer, 1993; Swales, 1990, pp. 43–58). Therefore, newcomers to a domain should be able to learn genres by encountering the purposes and conventions of the genres firsthand as well as by engaging in the social context of the domain, because genres are embedded in that context. Winsor (1996) espoused a similar view, arguing that students learn genres

through exposure to texts and to the genre knowledge they embody (p. 19). She also addressed the need for developing better understandings of how context affects rhetorical action (p. 42).

4. His introduction generally resembled the introductions for scientific research articles that rhetorical scholars have addressed. These scholars characterize such introductions as encapsulated problem-solution texts in which authors must continuously address and define the intellectual context of the discipline (Swales, 1990, p. 138; Swales & Najjar, 1987, pp. 178–179; Zappen, 1983, pp. 130–131). In the DOMC text, Bouzida addressed this context by positioning the physicists' work against other simulation work in biology, chemistry, and physics and by addressing how the physicists' own approach to conducting simulations moved beyond this previous work.

5. Although they are often unfamiliar with the tasks required of them, newcomers in mentoring-like relationships seldom are left entirely on their own to perform those tasks. Situated learning theorists use the notion of scaffolding to describe how experienced practitioners in a setting support newcomers as they begin to engage in the domain's activities. In their discussion of cognitive apprenticeships, for example, Brown et al. (1989) said, "Apprenticeship and coaching in a domain begin by providing modeling in situ and scaffolding for students to get started in an authentic activity" (p. 39). Collins et al. (1989) defined scaffolding as "the support, in the form of reminders and help, that the apprentice requires to approximate the execution of the entire composite of skills" (p. 456). Scaffolding, then, is support, provided as needed, to help newcomers to perform unfamiliar tasks. What is required for scaffolding to be effective, they said, "is accurate diagnosis of the student's current skill level or difficulty and the availability of an intermediate step at the appropriate level of difficulty in carrying out the target activity" (p. 482). This requirement bears similarities to Vygotsky's (1978) notion of the zone of proximal development, where the distance between a child's actual developmental level and that child's level of potential development is determined through problem-solving activity under the guidance of an adult or in collaboration with more capable peers (see also Brown & Palincsar, 1989, pp. 409–410). Furthermore, Vygotsky and scholars after him stressed that as the distance between the actual and potential developmental levels decreases, scaffolding can be reduced. Thus, the goal for the learner in such situations is autonomy in performing the modeled tasks. According to Lave and Wenger (1991), who used the notion of "legitimate peripheral participation" to describe such processes, newcomers begin their involvement in a domain at its periphery and then proceed inward toward more complete participation as they engage in the activities of the domain (p. 29). Lave and Wenger also accounted for the gradual reduction of support as newcomers begin to exhibit autonomy in their uses of modeled skills (pp. 95, 111).

6. Swendsen's concerns with not prescribing revisions for Bouzida are consistent with the beliefs of many situated learning theorists, who eschew prescription

and more intentional pedagogies for firsthand engagement in activities, such as the writing of scientific journal articles. Lave (1988), for example, said that the everyday activity that occurs in such situations is a more powerful source of socialization than intentional pedagogy (p. 14). In a similar vein, Collins et al. (1989) explained that the emphasis in apprenticeship-like relationships should be on observation, coaching, and successive approximation, not didactic teaching (p. 454). The comments of one physicist I interviewed even suggest that not being prescriptive can help students be more creative:

> The product might be better if students are left on their own—more originality, things that are clever, [and] certain better ways of doing things.... These things happen, so you don't want to turn off the creativity the person has in them. If you give them a prescription that's what you'll get back. You don't want to stifle them. (Bob, personal communication, May 1, 1991)

Prescriptive or cookbook approaches, Bob added, militate against such creativity. The flip side of these concerns, of course, is that such indirect support often seems insufficient to newcomers who have no previous experience engaging in the tasks they are asked to perform. That this may have been the case for Bouzida was suggested by the difficulties he had responding to Swendsen's feedback.

7. Ironically, Swendsen's own experiences with learning such tasks as a student were not unlike Bouzida's. Like Bouzida, Swendsen was also unaware of his advisor's intentions in regard to his professional and rhetorical learning. He once described his own experience at this stage, saying:

> My thesis advisor was a very good and clear writer. He's a good model. On the other hand, I'm not sure how much I learned or was aware of at the time. I wrote very slowly at the time, and it was—still is—very painful. I guess he did the same thing I'm doing now. He'd point out the impact things would have and what I could assume or not assume. It took quite a while to get through—it's been twenty years.... We didn't spend an awful lot of time writing things together, which is a shame because he writes very well. (personal communication, March 8, 1991)

Swendsen's advisor apparently used an approach similar to the one Swendsen used to transmit rhetorical skills to his students; however, Swendsen did not become conscious of this approach until much later in his career. In fact, his reflections during my study may have been what prompted Swendsen to recall and associate his advisor's efforts with professional and rhetorical instruction. Even with this awareness, however, Swendsen still did not make his approach for supporting Bouzida's learning any more explicit. Instead, his intentions remained unarticulated throughout the research and writing processes.

8. My observations of Bouzida's and Swendsen's interactions, along with my interviews with other physicists, indicate that the suggestive and inexplicit manner in which advisors often support their students may pose difficulties for them, especially

as they struggle to grasp the conceptual complexities entailed in composing discipline-specific genres. This finding is consistent with Freedman and Adam's (1996) findings regarding the difficulties newcomers often experience when they begin encountering such genres in the workplace. Freedman and Adam drew on Lave and Wenger's notion of legitimate peripheral participation to define a new notion—"attenuated authentic participation"—which described the often tacit and implicit character of learning in such circumstances: "The workplace operates as a community of practice whose tasks are focused on material or discursive outcomes and in which participants are often unaware of the learning that occurs" (p. 410). In Bouzida's case, this implicitness posed difficulties as he sought to understand and to apply the support Swendsen provided, and as he struggled to adequately address his audiences.

9. Bouzida's difficulties were especially apparent in his revisions to the early drafts and in Swendsen's responses to those revisions, which continued to focus on many of the same issues he addressed in the initial draft. For example, in response to the second draft, Swendsen again commented on the amount of technical information Bouzida had included and on his manner of arranging that information.

7

Sorting Out
Social Influences:
Distinguishing Authorial,
Audience, and Other Roles
in Scientific Work

In coming to a practical, experiential knowledge of audience, scientists may develop a conceptual vocabulary to identify the different levels and kinds of interactions they have with members of their audiences. If the writing is influenced by knowledge of and interaction with audience members, in a sense everyone with whom the scientist has had contact has a role in the writing. However, scientists, like Swendsen, who are largely concerned with ownership issues of accountability and rewards, clearly distinguish between significantly different kinds of participations in text production. Swendsen, in a depiction of such participations that he offered in response to one of my research accounts, emphasized the idea of the individual scientist who deserves and needs to be rewarded, a matter of understandable concern to Swendsen and to other scientists in their working lives. This depiction, which I present in this chapter, shows science marching forward in a linear manner, with Swendsen (or whoever is doing the publishing) hopefully on the cutting edge. It also shows scientific events to be ordered chronologically and hierarchically.

However, an alternative depiction, which I also offer in this chapter, rather than appearing well ordered like Swendsen's, shows how sequences of interactions and roles in science are fluid and recursive; for example, a person may act as a referee one moment and then change to the position of author whose work is subject to someone else's judgment. It also shows how people may make suggestions in hallway talk at a conference and then referee a paper in which their own suggestions are carried out (or rejected), or how a scientist may submit a paper to a referee who previously gave the scientist feedback on her ideas. This second depiction, which is based on the findings from my research, shows science as a more complexly communal activity in which it is hard to say who really thought of something first or proved it definitively, and thus as a community that has to develop mechanisms to authorize those decisions. It also shows, better than Swendsen's linear model, the dynamic and interactive character of various types of audience roles in science.

AUDIENCE MEMBERS AS COLLABORATORS

My findings from this research have led me to draw several conclusions about the physicists' composing activities and about the influence that their interactions with various members of their audiences had on those activities. In one report of these findings, published shortly after I completed my research, I labeled some of these interactions (specifically, those in which the physicists had engaged with David and George) *collaborations* (Blakeslee, 1993). I did this because of the extent to which these interactions had influenced the physicists' text. Had the physicists ignored these readers' feedback, the DOMC paper might have been deemed uncredible by their audiences in biology and chemistry (see chap. 5). In my earlier article, I summarized these perspectives, saying:

> During the initial stages of drafting the DOMC paper, the physicists engaged in a closed, tightly knit collaboration. However, when they decided to seek feedback from actual readers, they revealed the fluid boundaries of their collaboration by recruiting these readers to function first as reviewers and then as advisors, roles that changed in character when the readers questioned a central aspect of the physicists' presentation. The readers did not become co-authors, per se, but they influenced the physicists' inventive process, including the work being performed and the final written and visual formulations of the authors' knowledge claims.... They functioned as more than reviewers. (Blakeslee, 1993, p. 32)

My interpretation of these interactions in this case was based on a fairly broad definition of collaboration that included two aspects. First, like LeFevre (1987), I took as collaborative any influence of another, directly or indirectly, on the form and/or long-term meaning and consequences of a text. I also viewed such influence as occurring either concretely or in the imagination of the author. Furthermore, I viewed texts as having public lives both before and beyond the single act of composing and was concerned, therefore, with examining the complex social processes through which textual artifacts and meanings emerge in science. If we acknowledge such social influences as things to be encouraged, we arrive at the second aspect of my definition: that collaborativeness is a useful attitude to develop for all writers. In rhetoric, when we talk about collaboration from a pedagogical standpoint we usually conflate, to some degree, the processes of interaction described earlier and this attitude of collaborativeness that we wish to promote. Taken together, both aspects of this definition encourage consideration of several important questions; for example, who influences a text and its consequences? In what ways? And who wields little or no influence? Also, to what extent do individuals versus communities (or larger activity systems) create new knowledge? In this case the responses of some members of the physicists' audiences led the physicists to alter their DOMC text and their strategies for publicly positioning it (see chaps. 4 and 5).

AN ALTERNATIVE PERSPECTIVE

Although Swendsen also acknowledged that David's and George's responses influenced his group's work, he objected to my calling these influences collaborative. This was the only time that Swendsen ever challenged my interpretations of his group's activities. He did so, he said, because he disagreed with the inclusive manner in which I had defined and used this notion. He disagreed, in particular, with my taking as collaborative any influence of another on the form and/or long-term meaning and consequences of a text. From Swendsen's perspective, my designation of these activities as collaborative failed to discriminate sufficiently between the various interactions and influences that occurred here. In response to these objections, and with the aim of encouraging an ongoing dialogue with my informants, I requested two extended informal interviews with Swendsen after I had published the earlier article (see also, Blakeslee, Cole, & Conefrey, 1996a, 1996b). During these interviews I asked him to explain both his objections to my claims and his views on collaboration. I also asked him to characterize his interactions, both with Bouzida and Kumar, and with David and George. Here, I present Swendsen's perspectives on these interactions, and on various other factors, including audience, that may influence scientific authors.

A Different Definition of Collaboration

In contrast to my calling the physicists' interactions with David and George a collaboration, Swendsen offered a different interpretation. He said, first, that the primary reason he interacted with these scientists was to learn more about and to gauge the likely responses of his audiences:

> [David] was mirroring the presentation.... We were concerned [with] how people might read it.... This was going into a group that we didn't know that well, and there are assumptions we have made and we had to check them to find out what, what people thought of them. (personal communication, November 12, 1993)

As explained in chapter 3, Swendsen believed that he needed to interact directly with actual readers to develop an understanding of his audiences.

Swendsen also believed that such interactions were not collaborations. Although I defined collaboration as any influence that alters a scientist's work or text in a substantive manner, Swendsen defined it much more restrictively: "Collaboration is two or more people working together to do an experiment or to perform a calculation to solve a problem.... That's basically the distinction—having someone work with you to solve the problem" (personal communication, July 1, 1993). According to Swendsen, although David's and George's responses influenced their work and their presentation of that work in the DOMC paper, it did not contribute directly to solving the simulation problems the physicists were addressing: "The work was already done, and we wanted a response. [David] made the most important contribution but didn't actually help to solve the problem" (personal communication, July 1, 1993). Although potentially valuable, such a contribution, Swendsen went on to say, is not collaborative:

> In the course of a collaboration, or in the course of individual work, you'll often talk to other people, who will know something valuable or will, will bounce an idea off someone and say, "What do you think of this?" And they may make, may get valuable information, or you may get a valuable response, but that's not the same thing as collaboration, because they're not working on the problem with you. (personal communication, November 12, 1993)

Swendsen further distinguished collaborative and noncollaborative situations by drawing an analogy to a football team winning a game:

> I guess the analogy would be that ... if you have a football team, there is a specific group of people who are on the team, and they're the only ones who are on the team. Now to get at the contribution that the individual member of the team makes is of course influenced by all sorts of other stuff. It's happened to him in his training and how he grew up and his coaches he's been under and what other teams he has played on. But the only people on the team are this particular group.... So if the team wins, that's the group that gets credit for the win. I guess that's sort of what I'm saying. Now maybe the people in the stands cheering helped, but they're the readers. I mean maybe it does help ... definitely the coaches help, and they should get the credit for coaching but not for [actually playing the game and winning]. (personal communication, November 12, 1993)

Swendsen's analogy also shows a concern with distinguishing collaborators and noncollaborators—or authorial and audience roles, as in this case—for purposes of assigning credit.

In scientific publishing, the issue of credit is handled in various ways. According to Swendsen, those who collaborate in solving a problem are listed as co-authors on the papers the scientists produce: "If it's a successful collaboration and something actually comes about from it, then there's a paper that's written and [the] collaborators are co-authors on the paper" (personal communication, November 12, 1993). In contrast, those who simply provide input or contribute a useful idea to a paper are acknowledged in the notes at the end of the paper:

> If you have a conversation, let's say the conversation with David as an example. He wasn't a collaborator on this work, but he gave us valuable input in reaction to what we'd done. His purpose was not to solve the problem, and it wasn't, you know; what he said was not something that went towards solving the problem.... It was very valuable in terms of communication and telling us what our paper looked like and how it would be read. So that is something ... which we acknowledge under useful conversations, and, ah, so that will go into the acknowledgment of the paper as something useful in some way to the paper—through conversation. (personal communication, November 12, 1993)

Various types of involvements, for Swendsen, entail particular stances, activities, and roles in regard to scientific texts, as well as specific kinds of reward, blame, and personal responsibility. For this reason, when he elaborated his views on collaboration in our discussions, Swendsen was concerned, primarily, with distinguishing collaborators and noncollaborators so as to clarify their roles in the reward and responsibility system in science. According to Swendsen, decisions concerning promotion, tenure, and funding in science are made on the basis of what scientists contribute to their fields. Scientific advancement depends on the number of articles scientists publish, where they publish those articles (the prestige of the journals), and the success of the articles, usually determined through counts of citations. By suggesting that David and George were collaborators in the physicists' DOMC project, I had implied, according to Swendsen, that they should be rewarded in the same way and receive the same kind of credit as the three authors. However, these scientists had not contributed directly to the physicists' simulation work and therefore, according to Swendsen, they did not warrant such recognition. They simply were acting as audience members whom the physicists had asked to respond to the work.

In short, the contributions of David and George, according to Swendsen, were important to the physicists primarily insofar as they helped the authors to anticipate potential responses to their work from members of their audiences and to improve its chances of being accepted, particularly by biologists and chemists. Swendsen said such influences do not entail the same kind of commitment and responsibility, or the same kind of praise and blame in regard to the outcome of the text. (I would add, however, that such influences may entail other kinds of responsibility, such as ethical and professional reviewing, and professional honesty.) Therefore, what Swendsen objected to most when he saw how I had interpreted his interactions with these scientists was the inclusive manner in which I defined and used collaboration. He said, "There is a question of whether the definition is useful or not, and I don't think the definition that I'm hearing has, as being used in rhetoric, is useful because it's all-inclusive" (personal communication, November 12, 1993). He claimed that other scientists would also find such inclusiveness problematic. His comments also alerted me to issues relating to my own audiences:

> Well, you weren't addressing the paper to me. Your audience in this paper is not scientists. I think if you told me this was for publication in *Scientific American*, I would be, I would be quite surprised, and a bit upset, because I would, you know, foresee the flack you would get from scientists. Actually, I mean, when I think about it, I am surprised that the, that the word is used that widely without some other word being used in the, you know, to describe the more narrow classes. (personal communication, November 12, 1993)

When I reflected on these concerns and on my use of collaboration to cover all kinds of interactions, including interactions with audience members, I eventually became concerned with and critical of my own characterization. I realized that in rhetoric we tend to use the notion of collaboration broadly because there have not been enough studies that examine, up close, the social and public lives of texts both prior to and beyond the single act of composing. In other words, we may overclassify interactions as collaborative because we have not observed other interactions much and we do not know what else to do with them. We need to move away from simply labeling such interactions with just a single term.

Distinguishing Audience and Other Roles and Influences: A Spectrum of Interactions

In addition to raising concerns about how we conceive of different interactions in science, Swendsen also offered his perspectives on how to distinguish them. Specifically, as he discussed his views of collaboration in my interviews with him, Swendsen continued to clarify for me the kinds of contributions he believes scientists may make to a project. In doing so he suggested a map of participations and influences, a kind of representation of the scientific thought community, which I have tried to represent on the continuum in Fig. 7.1. In explicating this map, Swendsen emphasized the idea of the individual scientist deserving to be rewarded. He also depicted science as a fairly linear enterprise, with things happening in a mostly chronological and hierarchical order. Swendsen did useful work for us in this map by trying to make finer distinctions between interactions among various people than we usually draw. Specifically, he sequenced the roles and stances of audience members and other participants based on two characteristics: their potential impact on a project and their proximity to the main problem-solving tasks of the researchers. Swendsen's characterizations of these roles, which I elaborate in this section, suggest fairly predictable patterns of behavior that may well represent how science looks from the perspective of an insider, the working scientist.

In addition to distinguishing the various interactions that occur in scientific work, Swendsen also recommended generating new terms to characterize them. Such terms, he said, would allow us to better describe the interactions in which scientists engage in their work, along with the outcomes of those interactions:

> You know, if you had a different word to describe that, that would be less surprising to me. I mean, you've just got this all-inclusive word that distinguishes nothing and it seems it makes it more difficult to talk about what's going on. I would have been less surprised if you had 10 or 20 different, well, 5 or 10 different words to describe different kinds of interactions, distinctions that would clarify different kinds of relationships, which doesn't seem to be the case. (personal communication, November 12, 1993)

In describing and then calling for these additional terms to characterize scientists' interactions, Swendsen called attention to the multiplicity of roles and different kinds of agency that scientists may assume, both in their own and in each other's work. He sought to clarify the meanings of these roles in order to distinguish their contributions and to stabilize their places in the scientific reward system. Because *collaboration* has an important technical

Shoulders of Giants [Indirect contributions from previous work, education, & life experiences	Previously Published Work	Casual Conversa- tions with Other Scientists	Input from Advisors & Colleagues	Feedback from Seminars & Conferences	Requested Feedback	Reviewer & Editor Comments	Input from Peers & Co-Authors

FIG.7.1.   Participations and influences in the scientific thought community.

meaning in this system, Swendsen sought to clarify this meaning by bringing to light these many roles that may influence and occasion scientists' work.

An example may help to clarify Swendsen's perspectives. If a situation exists in which an editor is more deeply involved with and works harder on a manuscript than a tertiary author, the roles of these individuals, according to Swendsen, and their responsibility toward and for the text, are usually still distinct. These differences, Swendsen argued, need to be labeled, described, and clarified in order to arrive at a more accurate conception of the various kinds of participations and interactions that influence scientists. Swendsen's characterizations of some of these participations follow.

Shoulders of Giants. Swendsen, in constructing his map of participations, first described how the abstract and more indirect factors such as education, life experience, past work, and previous scientific achievements may contribute to a scientist's work. He used the "shoulders of giants" metaphor, which is a metaphor, derived from a statement by Isaac Newton, that scientists have used to describe their indebtedness to their predecessors. Swendsen said of these influences:

> It's assumed that all sorts of things go into the background of whatever your contribution was. I mean if I … write a paper and make some sort of a contribution, all kinds of things have gone into bringing me to this, to the level where I can make that contribution, including my entire education and my thesis advisor, and, you know, everybody I've worked with for many years. Without that … I wouldn't be here. I wouldn't be able to do what I can do. And some of it is more recent, you know, that there are conversations with various people to put me at that level. But then "I" have done something. OK. So everybody in the sciences is in that situation. We have, um, what is it they say? A euphemism I guess—"stood on the shoulders of giants." (personal communication, November 12, 1993)

Swendsen also described the impact of such influences—in particular his own previous research, background, and education—on his early work with the Monte Carlo method:

> Now, that step would not have been possible without our background in doing these simulations in the first place and then our work with what you can do with them and what the problems involved were. There are all sorts of people who contributed to my education in that. That's something I didn't even get into until after I had my Ph.D. People who helped educate me in that were not acknowledged in the paper because they didn't explicitly … contribute to that paper. They contributed to my getting to where I am. You can't put down everybody who has contributed to, back to my high school teacher who is a major influence on my papers.… There are … at least hundreds of people

who have contributed on that level. (personal communication, November 12, 1993)

Swendsen was referring in this quote to a project he had undertaken with a graduate student when he arrived at his current institution. His comments suggest the potential scope of such influences.

Swendsen's comments just given also echo some of Giddens's ideas. In Giddens's (1984) conceptions, influences lying just beneath an agent's level of consciousness (i.e., education, life experience, and past work) may guide the agent's actions. Giddens also addressed how the impact and consequences of an agent's actions are usually not limited to the immediate contexts of those actions (p. 11). He said that interactions and activities occurring in one time and place may influence subsequent interactions and activities, as well as the original interactions and activities (p. 14).[1] These ideas are supported by Swendsen's comments, here and in the next section, about the impact of scientific work over time. In general, then, Giddens's perspective provides a framework for considering the influence on the physicists of prior actions and ideas (their own and those of other scientists), the ways in which the physicists' ideas influenced members of their audiences, the impact of those ideas on the social life and structure of the communities they were targeting, and their impact even on the larger scientific enterprise.

Previous Scientific Work.   Swendsen used the project with his graduate student, which he described earlier, to define another type of influence on scientists—previous scientific work. First, however, he described how the project with his student originated:

> Shortly after I got here—I actually came with an idea and then we implemented that, I implemented it with a student of mine.... And this was ... an idea of how to do computer simulations in a very, in a radically different manner than had been done. Standard Monte Carlo was a method ... that had been developed for a long time, and we took a specific class of models and came up with a different way of doing it. It looked *very* different and was ... much more efficient for certain problems. (personal communication, November 12, 1993)

Because Swendsen viewed this student's contributions to his project as being fairly substantial, he listed him as a coauthor on the publication that resulted from this work. The student's name, which was Wong, also ended up being coupled with Swendsen's in other scientists' subsequent designation of the algorithm they had presented: "Now, when we wrote that up, that step of doing that became known as the Swendsen–Wong algorithm" (personal communication, November 12, 1993). This algorithm, Swendsen said, became their contribution to the field: "Nobody else was working on anything like that at the time, so we got credit for that step" (personal communication, November 12, 1993).

In discussing what had influenced this project, Swendsen described the previously published work of two scientists, which he said contributed significantly to how he and Wong performed their work:

> As an essential piece of being able to do that there was a paper by [two scientists] that had been written many years before. That was absolutely essential to what we did, and we acknowledged that very clearly—that the transformation we used in constructing our method was their transformation. We even put a derivation in that, in our paper explicitly that we labeled ... their transformation working somewhat differently so that you can see how our method springs from it. So they were acknowledged very explicitly with that. (personal communication, November 12, 1993)

Swendsen's comments show how previous scientific ideas become linked to new ideas in the construction of scientific knowledge. His comments also once again echo Giddens's ideas about the eventual impact and consequences of agents' actions and about the roles of those actions in transforming the larger activity systems in a domain.

Swendsen continued this illustration by describing how his and Wong's contributions from this work were eventually taken up and acknowledged by other scientists:

> So the step we took of going from ... what we knew generally about simulations, what the important problems were with simulations and ... then bringing in their transformation, that step of creating the method was ours. And we've been ... fully acknowledged in the literature that that was our step. (personal communication, November 12, 1993)

Swendsen also addressed the influence that their work had on scientists who read and used it in future work:

> After we did that, a number of people did a number of things based on that. For example, this guy ... from Germany. ... He introduced two other methods which would have been completely impossible without our work. So he ... read our work and then he did two other things. He's done more than two things, but there were two, you know, that primarily come out [of] ... that would have been impossible without our work. And yet they were things that we weren't thinking of at all that were acknowledged, you know, this is his contribution, a major contribution, a very important step. I wish I had thought of it. So he gets credit for that and then in his paper, he referenced ours. (personal communication, November 12, 1993)

The reciprocal processes of acknowledgment and credit that Swendsen describes here have been well documented by other scholars in the social studies of science (Blakeslee, 1994; Callon et al., 1986a; Carley & Kaufer, 1990; Cole, 1970; Kaufer & Carley, 1993; Latour, 1987; Law & Williams, 1982; Merton, 1968, 1973; Price, 1986). Swendsen's example, however, shows concretely how these vital processes perpetuate everyday scientific practice.

Informal and Formal Exchanges.   As Swendsen described the other influences in his spectrum, he commented next on the role and influence on scientific work of informal and formal interactions with colleagues. His comments on this category of interactions imply a more direct and concrete agency on the parts of interlocutors than that represented by the influences discussed thus far. He included in his characterization of these exchanges casual conversations with other scientists, solicited and unsolicited input from colleagues, and feedback from seminars and conferences. Of the more informal exchanges, such as those occurring in hallways, over lunch, and in colleagues' offices, he said:

> Another thing that happens quite frequently is that you just talk to somebody, maybe over lunch or walking in the hall, maybe actually spending the afternoon in somebody's office talking about it or about the background to a problem or something, but that's not the same as working on the problem. They're trying to understand the phenomena, and it may be valuable, and it's something that should always be acknowledged, but there's a distinction between that and working on the problem solving.... Now to some extent this is semantics, but I'm describing the usage within the scientific community. (personal communication, November 12, 1993)

In regard to how such interactions may contribute to a scientist's work, and the value of them, Swendsen added, "Conversations are extremely valuable. They can contribute something about some details of the background.... They help you clarify or correct some ideas in your mind" (personal communication, July 1, 1993). These were also the kinds of interactions that Swendsen and the other physicists I interviewed found valuable for learning about their audiences (see chap. 3).

When interactions such as these occur in settings that are more formal, such as at conferences, meetings, and colloquia, they can have an even greater impact on a scientist's work, according to Swendsen. In these more formalized settings, Swendsen said, scientists often encounter colleagues working on the same problem or on different aspects of that problem—essentially coworkers in their communities of practice. Thus, the scientists can discuss their respective projects and learn from each other. They can also use these occasions to try out their ideas and assumptions and to gauge potential responses to them:

There's also all kinds of feedback you get by giving papers and hearing papers at conferences. That was important in the conference I attended last week—what they understood or didn't understand, what they thought was important or not important. It was interesting, I was talking to someone Djamal was working with and he didn't understand one aspect of writing programs to do simulations. That's valuable in helping you know what you have to explain [to your audiences]. You also get an idea of what issues or ideas haven't been pursued. So, feedback in these cases becomes valuable in a number of ways. (personal communication, July 1, 1993)

In this instance the feedback Swendsen received helped him to identify and understand better a specific concern that a potential member of their audience had. The physicists actually used this strategy numerous times to learn about their audiences for the DOMC work (see chaps. 2 and 3).

Reviewing and Editing.   Other occasions for influence occur when scientific articles are reviewed and edited. In regard to how referees and editors can influence a project, Swendsen said that these individuals mirror for authors the eventual responses of audience members: "Sometimes that helps, sometimes you make a modification to the paper ... because the reviewer doesn't understand something, so you realize, 'Oh, I can't assume that,' or, 'I really forgot to put something in'" (personal communication, November 12, 1993). Swendsen also compared the feedback that referees typically provide with that provided by the scientists who responded to the DOMC paper:

The influence will often be quite similar to this feedback that [David] gave us about the, that plot. Usually not quite as substantial as that.... [pause] You know, something like, ah, "You didn't explain," or, "This explanation isn't sufficient," or, "Can you clarify," or, "You need another figure," or, "You can throw away two figures that are not necessary.... " Some journals ask for suggestions for shortening the paper. And sometimes you're asked to do that. Sometimes they're helpful suggestions, sometimes they're not. Having some feedback is valuable. (personal communication, November 12, 1993)

The biggest difference between the feedback audience members and referees offer, according to Swendsen, is that authors can more easily reject the feedback from audience members—these individuals can fail to cite an article, or cite it negatively, but referees can prevent the article from ever being published (Kaufer & Carley, 1993). Swendsen said the value of such authority is mixed: "Sometimes the reviewer will pick up something that, you know, is quite important and then it's very valuable to have, and sometimes reviewers will just miss the point completely and be a real pain in the neck" (personal communication, November 12, 1993).

In addressing formal reviews, Swendsen also commented on situations in which the feedback of referees significantly alters an author's work. In these cases, he said, the outcomes of the referees' feedback may warrant their acknowledgment as coauthors: "There have been cases of a paper going, being submitted for publication and the referee saying something so important, and changing the thrust of the paper that they, they have asked for the name of the referee for the purpose of putting it on the paper" (personal communication, November 12, 1993). Swendsen said that adding authors to a paper generally poses little difficulty, and therefore can be done easily (personal communication, November 12, 1993). Given Swendsen's concerns with distinguishing who is and is not a collaborator for the sake of recognition and reward, these comments seem surprising. However, he subsequently reiterated his belief that the boundaries of collaborations are not as fluid as these situations, which he now portrayed as uncommon, seem to suggest:

> It's very rare, but it, you know, it can happen that the referee will see something ... which is just really of major importance in changes, it's caused changes in conclusions or something. And the only appropriate thing is to ask the referee ... , you know, to make the change, but then you make the change in the paper and it's a far better paper, and you're much further along in solving things. Well, wait a minute, the referee did this, the referee should get ... credit.... This has happened. It's not, it's a very rare event, but it happens. (personal communication, November 12, 1993)

Although purportedly rare, situations such as these do suggest that referees may contribute something so significant to a scientist's work that they open the door for collaboration. However, Swendsen also noted that in such situations the referees' roles and responsibilities toward and for the scientific text remain distinct from those of the authors.

A more common event in science, according to Swendsen, is when authors ask prospective members of their audience to read an article before submitting it for publication, like the physicists did when they asked Ken, David, and George to read the DOMC paper. The feedback given in these cases, Swendsen said, can help authors to identify and correct problems that they may have overlooked: "It's rare that something will get by you and everybody else that you've shown it to" (personal communication, November 12, 1993). This feedback also helps authors to identify and correct any minor (or even major) problems that may exist in their texts:

> Usually ... there are small things that they'll point out—a reference, you know, that you've missed, and, ah, tell you the lettering in the figure is not clear, one paragraph isn't clear, or an explanation for something is missing, or you forgot to define something or other, or an equation is superfluous. Stuff like that. Those are the most common things that come up, which are valu-

able, but would not, in my mind, I mean I guess they would fit the collaboration definition that's used here, but certainly not mine. (personal communication, November 12, 1993)

Although he would not call such interactions collaborative, Swendsen, and other physicists I interviewed (e.g., David—see chap. 4), said that scientists often depend on such feedback prior to publishing their texts. Also, although the feedback in these cases is different from and carries less imperative than that offered by editors and reviewers, it may still involve issues of status and power. This was evidenced by both David's and George's responses and by the physicists' reactions to those responses.

Authorship and Credit.   As participations and interactions become more direct in science (moving linearly to the right of Swendsen's continuum), they eventually also raise questions about authorship and credit (Trimbur & Braun, 1992; Weber, 1991). Given Swendsen's beliefs that collaborations in science involve only those who contribute directly to solving a scientific problem, determining credit and authorship would seem easy. However, according to Swendsen, this is not always the case. Several factors, he said, can muddy such determinations. For example, in the field of biology, every scientist listed on the funding grant for a project becomes an author on all of the papers resulting from that project, even if their contributions to those papers are minimal. This disciplinary convention had a direct effect on the physicists when they wrote a paper on another aspect of their work, the multiple histogram method. They listed as authors for this paper two biologists who had not contributed to the research or to the writing. The physicists did this, they said, because these scientists were listed as coinvestigators on the original grant. Swendsen, with his strict conceptions of collaboration and of reward and responsibility in science, acknowledged his difficulties with this convention:

> With Chris, that was a problem. I wouldn't have listed him if I had been on my own. And Bob, ah ... I went along with Bob, and Ken, Ken would have been, Ken was sort of border because he made, he did make a lot of contributions, not as direct. So that was, that's ah, yeah, traditions in biology are different. I guess a little fuzzy. Now, the traditions are that everybody who was on the grant shares in the papers, and that's what we ran into here. So they have different traditions as to how to decide who's going to be on those papers, so that's why Ken's on it. (personal communication, November 12, 1993)

In contrast to situations like this one, Swendsen said that in condensed matter physics only those scientists who contribute to the actual work of the project are listed as authors. This illustrates how such definitions are also matters of communal convention.

Despite such occasional disciplinary complexities, Swendsen said that in most cases determining authorship and allocating credit for projects is easy. Further, making such determinations, according to Swendsen, is important for determining rewards and responsibilities in science, a belief that again emphasizes the idea of the individual scientist who needs and deserves to be rewarded: "Usually people can say fairly precisely what is it that was a particular person's or a particular group's contribution.... Maybe they can say it so precisely because getting credit for things is so important, and our reputation and promotion and tenure and all that stuff [depend on it]" (personal communication, November 12, 1993). Swendsen's perspectives reinforce that power in science is linked to persuasion, with key words like *reputation* serving as indicators of scientists' power. Intellectual discovery and progress in science appear to intertwine with or occur side by side with power and status relationships.

Somewhat less easy with regard to the question of authorship, according to Swendsen, is determining the ordering of authors on papers. Here conventions and practices vary, even within disciplines. Swendsen said, "That's complicated in science—that's really complicated. And the different subfields treat the question of the order of authors differently. And even when I go back and I look over what I've done and the decisions that I've been involved with ... it gets very difficult for me" (personal communication, November 12, 1993). Such determinations, he said, depend on several factors, including whether graduate students are involved in a project, and what contribution each individual has made to the work and to the paper. These concerns illustrate, once more, how such decisions depend on communal conventions.

As one example of how scientists determine who gets listed as an author, and in what order, Swendsen described the situations surrounding two papers he wrote with graduate students:

> The paper I was just describing, with the Swendsen–Wong algorithm, I put myself first because I had that idea before I came here, before I ever met him, and I had written a grant proposal that had it in it explicitly. That was mine. And then in the subsequent papers ... he became first author.... But the thing with Bouzida and Kumar, I guess it's actually an analogous situation, and I made a different decision that, because I did come up with the idea of this Dynamically Optimized Monte Carlo at Rutgers, and brought it back and explained it to them.... But Bouzida did all the work, all of it, with me looking over his shoulder, so I guess I felt that [it] was appropriate for him to take it. There's a tradition for the advisor to be the last author on the paper ... to put the graduate student first. (personal communication, November 12, 1993)

The tradition, or communal convention, Swendsen refers to in this quote is one that gives graduate students, who are new to the field, visibility and recognition. Swendsen said that it is not uncommon for senior scientists to manage grants and projects while their graduate students and postdoctoral fellows perform the day-to-day work of science, as was discussed in chapter 6. Therefore, their being listed as first authors, Swendsen said, is seldom questioned:

> If somebody comes along and has a lot of papers with students and the students are first author on everything, that's not really a problem. One of the things we're expected to do is to teach the students to author. So, it would be unusual if all of the work had the students as the first author, but that's quite possible, and that would not be looked down on. (personal communication, November 12, 1993)

Swendsen also said that scientists seldom mind listing their graduate students first on papers because first authorship is not as critical in science as it is in other fields. If there is any question about scientists' contributions to a project, he said, their colleagues and collaborators are simply asked about it:

> The paper is evidence that valuable work came out of the collaboration.... And then they go in and they ask specifically, "What has this person done?" ... So they go in and ask whoever worked on the project, whoever was in charge of the project, "What has this person done?" Then they give back an evaluation—"This person did something very important, this person was off gathering daisies." (personal communication, November 12, 1993)

Such practices once again suggest that interactions are the norm in this community and are used to support a number of activities.

In some situations, however, Swendsen acknowledged that questions of authorship may become important. For example, Swendsen said that in his area of theoretical physics the ordering of authors is important when coauthors are of comparable standing and rank. In these situations, he said, a scientist's failure to be listed as first author on any publications can be viewed as being problematic:

> If somebody never published ... say a theorist never publishes a paper at this point in his life, that can be a questionable case. And in that case it, it becomes very important to go back to the coauthors and ask why.... If you've got a lot of papers with colleagues and you're never first author, if ... if they're equals, then the person who contributed the most becomes first author, and then roughly in order. And if you're not first author there, you know, there's a question. If you never do anything that's not in collaboration, it's somebody else's, especially if that other person is very famous. (personal communication, November 12, 1993)

To illustrate his point further, Swendsen told the story of a scientist he knew who encountered this problem:

I know one guy in Germany who is extremely good. He spent a lot of his time collaborating with somebody else. His reputation isn't high now ... they've published 100 papers together, maybe more. Maybe 150 papers together. Superb work, but there was a little bit of a question of, well, to what extent is this guy riding on the other's coattails? As a matter of fact, I can think of a couple of cases where that's happened, where that question has been asked. In the cases that I know, where the question was raised, both people were extremely good, and I could now recognize them on their own, but it was something where it became important that they should stop collaborating with this person and go do something else to be recognized. You know, to be sure that they really could be famous on their own, or at least in collaboration with somebody else. (personal communication, November 12, 1993)

In this case Swendsen's comments suggest that, despite the seemingly widespread acceptance of certain authoring practices, the ordering of authors on scientific papers cannot always be taken for granted. Such ordering, at least in certain circumstances, is as important to scientists, and as problematic at times, as it is in the humanities. Again, reputation, power, and status are not insignificant.

Interdisciplinary Collaborations.   Swendsen also addressed in our discussions the special situations in which authors collaborate and engage in discursive interactions across disciplines, as the physicists were doing with the DOMC work. He said that in some areas of science, problems are so complex that they require input from scientists from a variety of specializations:

Problems in science tend to be complicated and there are many aspects of them. One of them is identifying the problem in the first place. The other is that to solve them you need many skills, and you may need more skills than one person has. Also, with people with the same skills, two or three people working together may be more effective [in helping you] get past certain stumbling blocks or sticking points [because of their] different points of view. (personal communication, July 1, 1993)

Swendsen said that in his field, condensed matter theory, interdisciplinary collaborations are valued because they indicate that the work has breadth. However, Swendsen also noted that in fields where more traditional views of science prevail, interdisciplinarity may be discouraged. He offered the following anecdote to illustrate such views:

I had a biochemist ask me how my work was viewed in the physics community because I had gone off into these other communities. He was surprised when I told him it was highly valued by my discipline and department. So, the attitudes might be different. I would suspect that going out of your field would be highly valued. I was surprised when he asked that question. (personal communication, July 1, 1993)

The biochemist's surprise in this case seems consistent with the trend toward specialization that has occurred historically in scientific development (Bledstein, 1976; Hagstrom, 1965; Paul & Blakeslee, 2000; Veysey, 1965).[2] However, interdisciplinary work, despite its difficulties, recently has begun to flourish and to figure prominently in much scientific research (Bowker, 1993; Gleick, 1987; Paul & Charney, 1995), a factor that may need to be addressed and taken more seriously in studies of collaboration and interactive dynamics in science.

A MODIFIED CONCEPTION

Swendsen's efforts to identify and distinguish authorial and audience roles, and collaborative and noncollaborative influences in science, contribute to our understanding of how interactions operate in and help to structure scientific communities and scientific knowledge. By mapping such interactions on a linear continuum, which I have represented and elaborated in this chapter, and by calling for a more refined semantic system to clarify these interactions, Swendsen called attention to the multiplicity of interactions and roles that function within the system of personal responsibility and reward in science. Swendsen distinguished these roles and interactions in terms of their proximity to the main tasks of science—solving problems and reporting results. In Swendsen's view, dialogic or interactional roles not directly entailed in the solving of scientific problems—such as those between authors and audience members when authors wish to obtain feedback on their work—are not collaborative, nor do they entail the same kind of responsibility as collaborative roles. However, Swendsen's views suggest that such roles are still essential.

Although I agree with Swendsen's concerns and objectives in identifying and distinguishing the various influences on a scientists' work, I also wish to modify his depiction of these influences. Although potentially useful, Swendsen's depiction, by representing scientific roles in hierarchical and linear terms, may limit our ability to account for the potentially fluid and shifting nature of these roles: for example, when reviewers become coauthors. As an alternative to this depiction, therefore, I wish to suggest a representation that accounts for the potential of participants to be more or less influential at various stages of a single project, or across several projects—a representation that acknowledges such variability, rather than assuming relatively stable roles located at predictable and measurable distances from scientific authors.

I present this modified representation in Fig. 7.2. (This depiction is provided here primarily for illustrative and suggestive purposes. It is not meant to be a comprehensive portrayal of the many participations and influences that may affect a scientist's work.) In constructing it, I had the same objectives as Swendsen:

- Clarifying the status of the interactions surrounding and contributing to a scientific project.
- Sorting out and distinguishing authorial and audience roles in a scientific endeavor.
- Preserving the technical value of the term *collaboration*.

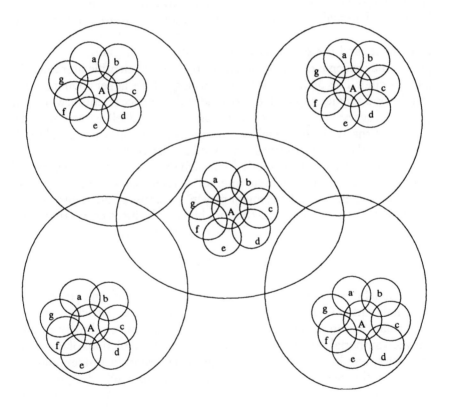

FIG. 7.2.   Participations and influences in scientific work—a more dynamic representation. Key: A, authors; a, reviewer–editor commentary; b, formal exchanges with colleagues; c, informal exchanges with colleagues; d, requested feedback; e, previous scientific work; f, education and experience; g, past scientific achievement.

I have tried to address these objectives by displaying a variety of interactions, which Swendsen also does, and by portraying these interactions through the use of overlapping and open circles, a departure from Swendsen. These overlapping and open circles, which I place at equal distances from the circle in which I locate the authors, are meant to suggest the fluid and flexible boundaries that may exist between participants and authors, and even between participants. My depiction thus shows how the sequences of roles and interactions in science are fluid and recursive, and it depicts science as a more complexly communal activity in which it may be difficult to say in every case who really thought of something first or proved it definitively.

Implicit in my modified design, also, is the potential for participants to have more or less influence on authors and to shift and relocate themselves at different stages of a project (e.g., authors may interact with the same colleagues both formally and informally at different points during a project, referees may have heard the scientists' work previously at a seminar or conference, and the scientists whom authors consult informally during a project may become reviewers or may be part of the scientific literature the authors cite). This design is also meant to suggest the larger communal enterprise and activity system that surround and influence scientific work. It is meant to suggest and reinforce the self-organizing and self-perpetuating dynamics of the scientific social system, implying, perhaps more indirectly than explicitly, the connections that exist between scientific agency and social structure (see Giddens, 1984).[3] Through this more dynamic depiction I hope to account for the multiple interactive roles that various individuals, including audience members, might play in a scientist's work. I also hope to account for both the range and the variability of the interactions that influence change and the creation of knowledge in science.

CONCLUSION

I have sought in this final chapter to give voice to Swendsen's perspectives on collaboration and to his perspectives on the various participations and roles that occur in scientific work—including his views on the distinctions between authorial and audience roles. I present two depictions of these various roles, one based on Swendsen's perspectives as an insider, and one based on the perspectives I gained from my research. In presenting Swendsen's depiction, I show how Swendsen was concerned with clarifying participants' roles and influences so as to stabilize their place in the scientific reward system. In his characterizations of these influences, he attributed certain predictable roles and statuses to participants, such as referees, based on their usual contributions to projects. For Swendsen, these roles remain relatively stable, carrying a more-or-less constant and predictable weight in the scientific authoring and reward system. In contrast, my own depiction of these influences, which is more fluid, tries to capture the dynamic and recursive nature of these influences. My examination in my research of the social life of the DOMC text, and my subsequent discussions with Swendsen, allowed me to conceive of these interactive dynamics in more ways than the single term *collaboration* permits. By identifying and describing various influences, and not just calling them collaborative in the most general sense, we develop a better understanding of the complex social processes that inevitably surround and influence the production of scientific texts and knowledge. We also develop a better understanding of the various ways in which audience members and other individuals may function in and influence a scientists' work.

NOTES

1. Giddens (1984) said that beyond their immediate contexts, actions may have unintended consequences that may affect further conditions of action in the original context:

> Repetitive activities, located in one context of time and space, have regularized consequences, unintended by those who engage in those activities, in more or less "distant" time–space contexts. What happens in this second series of contexts then, directly or indirectly influences the further conditions of action in the original context. (p. 14)

Giddens also pointed out that because agents' purposive actions have such unintended consequences, social life is not always an intentional product of its constituent actors (p. 343).

2. It may have also stemmed from a sense of physics as a colonizing field, one that provides "fundamental" theories and tools to other fields, but that asserts that physics, after all, is really what it is all about.

3. These ideas are not portrayed very explicitly in my map because of both practical drawing constraints and their abstract quality; however, they are important to acknowledge in our examinations of scientific work and its social and communal underpinnings.

Afterword

Throughout this book, I have contributed to our understanding of audience and of the roles audience members may play in scientific work. Mine is the first long-term, empirical study of how scientific authors, situated in communities of practice among heterogeneous coactors, learn about and address their audiences. By examining how the physicists planned and prepared their texts, and by looking at the various social and rhetorical activities that constituted their everyday practice, my work shows how successful writers continually adjust their rhetorical strategies to adapt to both barriers and opportunities posed by their interlocutors. It also provides a better understanding of how audience members and other individuals may function in and influence a scientist's work.

One area my research makes clear is the dynamic and interactive nature of audience knowledge. This dynamic view of audience, which is supported throughout this book, contrasts with the more static views that we have assumed and relied on for so long, both in composition studies more generally and in the rhetoric of science more particularly. Such static views have been reinforced by our tendency, especially in studies of science, to focus primarily on written products. In particular, scholars in composition have tended to view audience from the perspective of authors and the texts they create. Scholars in the rhetoric of science have done the same, often focusing on historically significant scientific works rather than examining the various rhetorical strategies scientists use in the works they are currently developing. Most rhetorical perspectives on audiences thus conceptualize them as passive consumers of the information directed toward them. Such perspectives also support a view of rhetoric as a construct that authors use to control audiences. Authors, concerned with manipulating and dominating their audiences, are portrayed as making distant guesses about them based on assumptions and broad-stroke characterizations. However, an examination of those products while they are still in the making reveals the multiple inter-active processes by which authors get to know and speak to their audiences, along with the difficulties inherent in those processes.

As a specific example of this, audience, for the physicists, was far from a transparent or unproblematic phenomenon. Swendsen, Bouzida, and Kumar expended a great deal of energy learning about their audiences. They were responsive to the contingencies of audience, making local, improv-isatory rhetorical decisions that ultimately impacted the shape of their work and who it reached. They deliberately planned and carried out various strat-egies, from the initial stages of their work to beyond its publication, to influ-ence and persuade their constituents.

Thus, I was able to get in this research at the role of interaction in audi-ence knowledge and how such interaction is ongoing. My findings show how scientists rely on direct interactions with actual audience members to obtain information about their audiences and to address their concerns. (Familiar-ity allows an author to write to an audience with ease because he or she knows the majority of the audience personally.) These findings suggest viewing audience as a real, physical entity that authors can interact with and come to know (and be influenced by) on a more direct and personal level, an entity that is not abstract and static, but dynamic and fluid. Audiences are real entities that can be addressed and made more concrete and discernible. Such findings thus suggest that writing is a social process that involves envi-sioned as well as real, interactionally experienced audiences. Authors' un-derstanding of and approaches to audience rest on a continuum someplace between imagined and real.

My observations of the physicists also suggest a model for audience analy-sis in which authors interact with audience members to determine how they might respond to their ideas and how, therefore, they should present their ideas given their audiences' attitudes and potential responses. This model thus consists of two primary operations: (a) getting to know and understand one's interlocutors, and (b) determining how to reach and influence them. These are the two operations that need to occur, and interaction is constitu-tive of both. This model also supports thinking of audience analysis as a dy-namic activity—ongoing interaction allows authors to monitor and keep track of the changing concerns of audiences. Such a model, however, may also need to be qualified. For example, Swendsen, Bouzida, and Kumar made trade-offs because of time and other constraints; thus, the concerns they expressed for their audiences were not always the same as doing what it would take to bridge the gap successfully between themselves and their un-familiar interlocutors. My findings suggest that authors may apportion time and attention in particular writing situations, which can have an impact on how ideas are shaped and organized, as well as on outcomes. Authors' inter-

actions with audiences are thus affected by such issues as time and efficiency, willingness and capability to change, ethos and status, genre and
type of acceptance sought, duration and intensity or depth of experience
within one's own or a different community, and inherent skill.

The primary aim of this work was to help us develop a more realistic sense
of how scientific authors interact with their audiences. However, the issues
at stake really apply to all communication. For example, looking at how the
physicists tried to cope with a limited amount of information about their audience provides a perspective on the real and difficult issues of how authors,
more generally, get to know and speak to an audience. Audiences are complex entities that require strategic, lifelong learning rather than one-time
mastery. Every physicist in my study was concerned with fostering ongoing
relationships with members of their audiences and with not restricting such
encounters to a single rhetorical episode—their actions revealed an awareness of both the immediate and the longer term contexts for their work.
They felt the need to participate directly in the communities they were addressing and to engage in ongoing interactions with the members of those
communities. The social immersion they described has as its aim initiation
into the conversation of the community one wishes to address, whether that
community is one's own or a new and unfamiliar community.

In summary, my work suggests an alternative view of audience based on
cooperative interaction between authors and their interlocutors. The conclusions I draw in this work include the following:

- Distant guesses about audience based on assumptions about uniformity or
  broad-stroke characterizations aimed at manipulation and domination rather
  than cooperative interaction don't work well.
- Intimate, interactive knowledge of audiences pushes authors to stronger,
  more effective arguments. Longer term immersion and face-to-face interaction with actual members of a domain can push authors past stereotypical
  positionings.
- Real, functional knowledge of audience comes only over time by entering into
  some community of practice.
- To persuade and gain support for their ideas, scientists must determine how to
  target and appeal to their audience. Interaction plays a seminal role in these
  processes.

Although these conclusions are important, they are still just a beginning.
As I stated in chapter 1, my hope is that studies like mine will lead to further
investigations of these interactions and processes, which are vital to our understanding of audience. Such investigations might focus on any of a number of issues. For example, scholars might examine how authors (in science

as well as in other domains) acquire, cope with, and respond to information about their audiences; how authors are socialized into various disciplines (how both newcomers and experienced practitioners get to know their interlocutors in particular communities); and how authors may apportion time and attention as they learn about and try to reach their audiences. To move away from views in which authors dominate and control audiences, scholars need to examine, up close, the interactions in which authors engage with their audiences throughout their work. They need to study authors as they plan, compose, and position their work. In summary, by broadening their perspectives on audience, rhetorical scholars can understand better how authors interact with and come to know (and are influenced by) audiences directly and personally.

References

Bazerman, C. (1981). What written knowledge does: Three examples of academic discourse. *Philosophy of the Social Sciences, 11*, 361–387.

Bazerman, C. (1984a). Modern evolution of the experimental report in Physics: Spectroscopic articles in *Physical Review*, 1893–1980. *Social Studies of Science, 14*, 163–196.

Bazerman, C. (1984b). The writing of scientific non-fiction: Contexts, choices, and constraints. *PRE/TEXT, 5*, 39–74.

Bazerman, C. (1985). Physicists reading physics: Schema-laden purposes and purpose-laden schema. *Written Communication, 2*, 3–23.

Bazerman, C. (1988). *Shaping written knowledge: The genre and activity of the experimental article in science*. Madison: University of Wisconsin Press.

Bazerman, C. (1994). Systems of genres and the enactment of social intentions. In A. Freedman & P. Medway (Eds.), *Genre and the new rhetoric* (pp. 79–101). London: Taylor & Francis.

Bereiter, C., & Scardamalia, M. (1987). *The psychology of written composition*. Hillsdale, NJ: Lawrence Erlbaum Associates.

Berkenkotter, C. (1981). Understanding a writer's awareness of audience. *College Composition and Communication, 32*, 388–399.

Berkenkotter, C., & Huckin, T. N. (1995). *Genre knowledge in disciplinary communication: Cognition/culture/power*. Hillsdale, NJ: Lawrence Erlbaum Associates.

Bitzer, L. F. (1968). The rhetorical situation. *Philosophy and Rhetoric, 1*, 1–14.

Blakeslee, A. M. (1992). *Inventing scientific discourse: Dimensions of rhetorical knowledge in physics*. Unpublished doctoral dissertation, Carnegie Mellon University, Pittsburgh, PA.

Blakeslee, A. M. (1993). Readers and authors: Fictionalized constructs or dynamic collaborations? *Technical Communication Quarterly, 2*, 23–35.

Blakeslee, A. M. (1994). The rhetorical construction of novelty: Presenting claims in a letters forum. *Science, Technology, & Human Values, 1*, 88–100.

Blakeslee, A. M. (1997). Activity, context, interaction, and authority: Learning to write scientific papers in situ. *Journal of Business and Technical Communication, 11*, 125–169.

Blakeslee, A. M., Cole, C. M., & Conefrey, T. (1996a). Constructing voices in writing research: Developing participatory approaches to situated inquiry. In G. Kirsch & P. Mortensen (Eds.), *Ethics and representation in qualitative studies of literacy* (pp. 134–154). Urbana, IL: NCTE.

Blakeslee A. M., Cole, C. M., & Conefrey, T. (1996b). Evaluating qualitative inquiry in technical and scientific communication: Toward a practical and dialogic validity. *Technical Communication Quarterly, 5*, 125–149.

Bledstein, B. J. (1976). *The culture of professionalism: The middle class and the development of higher education in America*. New York: Norton.

Bouzida, D., Kumar, S., & Swendsen, R. H. (1991). Almost Markov processes. *Springer Proceedings in Physics, 53*, 193–196.

Bouzida, D., Kumar, S., & Swendsen, R. H. (1992). Efficient Monte Carlo methods for the computer simulation of biological molecules. *Physical Review D, 45*, 8894–8901.

Bowker, G. (1993). How to be universal: Some cybernetic strategies, 1943–70. *Social Studies of Science, 23*, 107–127.

Brandt, D. (1990). *Literacy as involvement: The acts of writers, readers, and texts*. Carbondale: Southern Illinois University Press.

Brown, A. L., & Palincsar, A. S. (1989). Guided, cooperative learning and individual knowledge acquisition. In L. B. Resnick (Ed.), *Knowing, learning, and instruction: Essays in honor of Robert Glaser* (pp. 393–451). Hillsdale, NJ: Lawrence Erlbaum Associates.

Brown, J. S., Collins, A., & Duguid, P. (1989). Situated cognition and the culture of learning. *Educational Researcher, 18*, 32–42.

Burke, P. B. (1967). Rhetorical considerations of Bacon's "style." *College Composition and Communication, 18*, 23–30.

Callon, M., Law, J., & Rip, A. (Eds.). (1986a). *Mapping the dynamics of science and technology: Sociology of science in the real world*. Houndsmills, Basingstoke, Hampshire: Macmillan.

Callon, M., Law, J., & Rip, A. (1986b). How to study the force of science. In M. Callon, J. Law & A. Rip (Eds.), *Mapping the dynamics of science and technology: Sociology of science in the real world* (pp. 3–15). Houndsmills, Basingstoke, Hampshire: Macmillan.

Campbell, J. A. (1975). The polemical Mr. Darwin. *Quarterly Journal of Speech, 61*, 375–390.

Campbell, J. A. (1989). The invisible rhetorician: Charles Darwin's "third party" strategy. *Rhetorica, 7*, 55–85.

Carley, K., & Kaufer, D. (1990). *Factoring the reach of a scientific paper*. Paper presented at the annual conference of the Society for the Social Studies of Science, October, Minneapolis, MN.

Chandhok, R., Morris, J., Kaufer, D., & Neuwirth, C. (1992). Prep Editor. (Version 1.0d39, Computer software). Apple Macintosh, 8 MB, disk. Pittsburgh, PA: Carnegie Mellon University.

Chandhok R., Morris, J., Kaufer, D., & Neuwirth, C. (1996). Commonspace. (Version 1.1, Computer software). Cross platform, 8 MB, disk. Boston: Houghton Mifflin, Sixth Floor Media.

Charney, D. (1993). A study in rhetorical reading: How evolutionists read "The Spandrels of San Marco." In J. Selzer (Ed.), *Understanding scientific prose* (pp. 203–231). Madison: University of Wisconsin Press.

Cole, S. (1970). Professional standing and the reception of scientific discoveries. *American Journal of Sociology, 76*, 286–306.

Collins, A., Brown, J. S., & Newman, S. E. (1989). Cognitive apprenticeship: Teaching the crafts of reading, writing, and mathematics. In L. B. Resnick (Ed.), *Knowing, learning, and instruction: Essays in honor of Robert Glaser* (pp. 453–494). Hillsdale, NJ: Lawrence Erlbaum Associates.

Committee on the Conduct of Science, National Academy of Sciences (1989). *On being a scientist*. Washington, DC: National Academy Press.

Crane, D. (1972). *Invisible colleges: Diffusion of knowledge in scientific communities*. Chicago, IL: University of Chicago Press.

Crinsmore, A., & Farnsworth, R. (1989). Mr. Darwin and his readers: Exploring interpersonal metadiscourse as a dimension of ethos. *Rhetoric Review, 8*, 91–111.

Daniel, S. H. (1982). Myth and the grammar of discovery in Francis Bacon. *Philosophy and Rhetoric, 15*, 219–237.

Doheny-Farina, S. (1992). *Rhetoric, innovation, technology: Case studies of technical communication in technology transfers*. Cambridge, MA: MIT Press.

Ede, L., & Lunsford, A. (1984). Audience addressed/audience invoked: The role of audience in composition theory and pedagogy. *College Composition and Communication, 35*, 155–171.

Elbow, P. (1987). Closing my eyes as I speak: An argument for ignoring audience. *College English, 49*, 50–69.

Fahnestock, J. (1986). Accommodating science: The rhetorical life of scientific facts. *Written Communication, 3*, 275–296.

Fahnestock, J., & Secor, M. (1988). The stases in scientific and literary argument. *Written Communication, 5*, 427–443.

Freedman, A., & Adam, C. (1996). Learning to write professionally: "Situated learning" and the transition from university to professional discourse. *Journal of Business and Technical Communication, 10*, 395–427.

Garvey, W. (1979). *Communication: The essence of science*. Oxford: Pergamon.

Giddens, A. (1984). *The constitution of society: Outline of the theory of structuration*. Berkeley: University of California Press.

Gieryn, T. F. (1978). Problem retention and problem change in science. In J. Gaston (Ed.), *Sociology of science* (pp. 96–115). San Francisco: Jossey-Bass.

Gleick, J. (1987). *Chaos: Making a new science*. New York: Penguin.

Gragson, G., & Selzer, J. (1990). Fictionalizing the readers of scholarly articles in biology. *Written Communication, 7*, 25–58.

Gross, A. G. (1988). Discourse on method: The rhetorical analysis of scientific texts. *PRE/TEXT, 3–4*, 169–185.

Gross, A. (1990). *The rhetoric of science: The rhetorical analysis of scientific texts*. Cambridge, MA: Harvard University Press.

Haas, C. (1994). Learning to read biology: One student's rhetorical development in college. *Written Communication, 11*, 43–84.

Haas, C., & Flower, L. (1988). Rhetorical reading strategies and the construction of meaning. *College Composition and Communication, 39*, 167–183.

Hagstrom, W. O. (1965). *The scientific community*. New York: Basic Books.

Halloran, S. M. (1978). Technical writing and the rhetoric of science. *Journal of Technical Writing and Communication, 8*, 77–88.

Halloran, S. M. (1984). The birth of molecular biology: An essay in the rhetorical criticism of scientific discourse. *Rhetoric Review, 3*, 70–82.

Halloran, S. M., & Whitburn, M. D. (1982). Ciceronian rhetoric and the rise of science: The plain style reconsidered. In J. J. Murphy (Ed.), *The rhetorical tradition and modern writing* (pp. 58–72). New York: MLA.

Johnson, R. R. (1997). Audience involved: Toward a participatory model of writing. *Computers and Composition, 14*, 361–376.

Journet, D. (1990). Forms of discourse and the sciences of the mind: Luria, Sacks, and the role of narrative in neurological case histories. *Written Communication, 7*, 171–199.

Kaufer, D. S., & Carley, K. M. (1993). *Communication at a distance: The influence of print on sociocultural organization and change*. Hillsdale, NJ: Lawrence Erlbaum Associates.

Kinneavy, J. L. (1971). *A theory of discourse: The aims of discourse*. New York: Norton.

Kirsch, G., & Roen, D. H. (Eds.). (1990). *A sense of audience in written communication. Written communication annual: An international survey of research and theory* (vol. 5). Newbury Park, CA: Sage.

Knorr, K. D. (1979). Tinkering toward success: Prelude to a theory of scientific practice. *Theory and Society, 8*, 347–376.

Knorr-Cetina, K. (1981). *The manufacture of knowledge: An essay on the constructivist and contextual nature of science*. Oxford: Pergamon.

Krauss, R. M., & Fussell, S. R. (1990). Mutual knowledge and communicative effectiveness. In J. Galegher, R. E. Kraut & C. Egido (Eds.), *Intellectual teamwork: Social and technological foundations of cooperative work* (pp. 111–145). Hillsdale, NJ: Lawrence Erlbaum Associates.

Kronick, D. A. (1976). *A history of scientific and technical periodicals: The origin and development of the scientific and technical press, 1665–1790* (2nd ed.). Metuchen, NJ: Scarecrow Press.

Latour, B. (1987). *Science in action: How to follow scientists and engineers through society*. Cambridge, MA: Harvard University Press.

Latour, B., & Woolgar S. (1986). *Laboratory life: The construction of scientific facts*. Princeton, NJ: Princeton University Press.

Lave, J. (1988). *Cognition in practice: Mind, mathematics and culture in everyday life*. Cambridge, England: Cambridge University Press.

Lave, J., & Wenger, E. (1991). *Situated learning: Legitimate peripheral participation*. Cambridge: Cambridge University Press.

Law, J. (1986). The heterogeneity of texts. In M. Callon, J. Law & A. Rip (Eds.), *Mapping the dynamics of science and technology* (pp. 67–83). Houndsmills, Basingstoke, Hampshire: Macmillan.

Law, J., & Williams, R. (1982). Putting facts together: A study in scientific persuasion. *Social Studies of Science, 12*, 535–558.

LeFevre, K. B. (1987). *Invention as a social act*. Carbondale: Southern Illinois University Press.

Lipson, C. S. (1985). Francis Bacon and plain scientific prose: A reexamination. *Journal of Technical Writing and Communication, 15*, 143–155.

Long, R. (1980). Writer–audience relationships: Analysis or invention? *College Composition and Communication, 31*, 221–226.

Long, R. C. (1990). The writer's audience: Fact or fiction? In G. Kirsch & D. H. Roen (Eds.), *A sense of audience in written communication*. *Written communication annual: An international survey of research and theory* (vol. 5; pp. 73–84). Newbury Park, CA: Sage.

McCloskey, D. N. (1985). *The rhetoric of economics*. Madison: University of Wisconsin Press.

Merton, R. K. (1968). The Matthew effect in science. *Science, 159*, 56–63.

Merton, R. K. (Ed.). (1973). *The sociology of science: Theoretical and empirical investigations*. Chicago, IL: University of Chicago Press.

Merton, R. K., & Zuckerman, H. (1973). Institutionalized patterns of evaluation in science. In R. K. Merton (Ed.), *The sociology of science: Theoretical and empirical investigations* (pp. 460–496). Chicago, IL: University of Chicago Press.

Miller, C. R. (1984). Genre as social action. *Quarterly Journal of Speech, 70*, 151–176.

Miller, C. R. (1992). *Kairos* in the rhetoric of science. In S. P. Witte, N. Nakadate & R. D. Cherry (Eds.), *A rhetoric of doing: Essays on written discourse in honor of James L. Kinneavy* (pp. 310–327). Carbondale: Southern Illinois University Press.

Mishler, E. (1990). Validation in inquiry-guided research: The role of exemplars in narrative studies. *Harvard Education Review, 4*, 415–442.

Moran, M. C. (1984). Joseph Priestley, William Duncan, and analytic arrangement in eighteenth-century scientific discourse. *Journal of Technical Writing and Communication, 14*, 207–215.

Myers, G. (1985). The social construction of two biologists' proposals. *Written Communication, 2*, 219–245.

Myers, G. (1989). The pragmatics of politeness in scientific articles. *Applied Linguistics, 10*, 1–35.

Myers, G. (1990). *Writing biology: Texts in the social construction of scientific knowledge*. Madison: University of Wisconsin Press.

Myers, G. (1991). Stories and styles in two molecular biology review articles. In C. Bazerman & J. Paradis (Eds.), *Textual dynamics of the professions: Historical and contemporary studies of writing in professional communities* (pp. 45–75). Madison: University of Wisconsin Press.

Myers, G. (1996). Out of the laboratory and down to the bay: Writing in science and technology studies. *Written Communication*, 13, 5–43.

Ong, W. J. (1975). The writer's audience is always a fiction. *PMLA*, 90, 9–21.

Paradis, J. (1983). Bacon, Linnaeus, and Lavoisier: Early language reform in the sciences. In P. V. Anderson, R. J. Brockmann & C. R. Miller (Eds.), *New essays in technical and scientific communication: Research, theory, and practice* (pp. 200–224). Farmingdale, NY: Baywood.

Park, D. B. (1982). The meaning of audience. *College English*, 44, 247–257.

Paul, D., & Blakeslee, A. M. (2000). Inventing the American research university: Nineteenth-century American science and the new middle class. In M. Goggin (Ed.), *Inventing a discipline, rhetoric and composition in action: Essays in honor or Richard E. Young*. Urbana, IL: NCTE.

Paul, D., & Charney, D. (1995). Introducing chaos (theory) into science and engineering: Effects of rhetorical strategies on scientific readers. *Written Communication*, 12, 396–438.

Perelman, C., & Olbrechts-Tyteca, L. (1969). *The new rhetoric: A treatise on argumentation* (J. Wilkenson & P. Weaver, Trans.). Notre Dame, IN: University of Notre Dame Press.

Porter, J. E. (1992). *Audience and rhetoric: An archaeological composition of the discourse community*. Englewood Cliffs, NJ: Prentice Hall.

Prelli, L. J. (1989). *A rhetoric of science: Inventing scientific discourse*. Columbia: University of South Carolina Press.

Price, D. de S. (1986). *Little science, big science ... and beyond*. New York: Columbia University Press.

Rafoth, B. A. (1989). Audience and information. *Research in the Teaching of English*, 23, 273–290.

Reeves, C. (1990). Establishing a phenomenon: The rhetoric of early medical reports on AIDS. *Written Communication*, 7, 393–416.

Roen, D. H., & Willey, R. H. (1988). The effects of audience awareness on drafting and revising. *Research in the Teaching of English*, 22, 75–88.

Roth, R. G. (1987). The evolving audience: Alternatives to audience accommodation. *College Composition and Communication*, 38, 47–55.

Russell, D. R. (1997). Rethinking genre in school and society: An activity theory analysis. *Written Communication*, 14, 504–554.

Rymer, J. (1988). Scientific composing processes: How eminent scientists write journal articles. In D. A. Jolliffe (Ed.), *Advances in writing research: Vol. 2. Writing in academic disciplines* (pp. 211–250). Norwood, NJ: Ablex.

Schriver, K. A. (1997). *Dynamics in document design: Creating text for readers*. New York: Wiley.

Schryer, C. F. (1993). Records as genres. *Written Communication*, 10, 200–234.

Selzer, J. (1992). More meanings of audience. In S. P. Witte, N. Nakadate & R. D. Cherry (Eds.), *A rhetoric of doing: Essays on written discourse in honor of James L. Kinneavy* (pp. 161–177). Carbondale: Southern Illinois University Press.

Selzer, J. (Ed.). (1993). *Understanding scientific prose*. Madison: University of Wisconsin Press.

Spilka, R. (1988a). *Adapting discourse to multiple audiences: Invention strategies of seven corporate engineers*. Unpublished doctoral dissertation, Carnegie Mellon University, Pittsburgh, PA.

Spilka, R. (1988b). Studying writer–reader interactions in the workplace. *The Technical Writing Teacher*, 15, 208–221.

Spilka, R. (1990). Orality and literacy in the workplace: Process- and text-based strategies for multiple audience adaptation. *Journal of Business and Technical Communication*, 4, 44–67.

Stephens, J. (1975). Rhetorical problems in Renaissance science. *Philosophy and Rhetoric*, 8, 213–229.

Stephens, J. (1983). Style as therapy in Renaissance science. In P. Anderson, R. J. Brockmann & C. R. Miller (Eds.), *New essays in technical and scientific communication: Research, theory, and practice* (pp. 187–199). Farmingdale, NY: Baywood.

Sullivan, D. (1996). Displaying disciplinarity. *Written Communication*, *13*, 221–250.

Swales, J. M. (1990). *Genre analysis: English in academic and research settings*. Cambridge: Cambridge University Press.

Swales, J., & Najjar, H. (1987). The writing of research article introductions. *Written Communication*, *4*, 175–191.

Thacker, B., & Stratman, J. F. (1995). Transmuting common substances: The cold fusion controversy and the rhetoric of science. *Journal of Business and Technical Communication*, *9*, 389–424.

Traweek, S. (1992). Border crossings: Narrative strategies in science studies among physicists in Tsukuba Science City, Japan. In A. Pickering (Ed.), *Science as practice and culture* (pp. 429–465). Chicago, IL: University of Chicago Press.

Trimbur, J., & Braun, L. A. (1992). Laboratory life and the determination of authorship. In J. Forman (Ed.), *New visions of collaborative writing* (pp. 19–36). Portsmouth, NH: Boynton/Cook.

Veysey, L. R. (1965). *The emergence of the American university*. Chicago, IL: University of Chicago Press.

Vygotsky, L. S. (1978). *Mind in society: The development of higher psychological processes*. M. Cole, V. John-Steiner, S. Scribner & E. Souberman (Eds.). Cambridge, MA: Harvard University Press.

Weber, J. R. (1991). The construction of multi-authored texts in one laboratory setting. In M. M. Lay & W. M. Karis (Eds.), *Collaborative writing in industry: Investigations in theory and practice* (pp. 49–63). Amityville, NY: Baywood.

White, J. B. (1985). *Heracle's bow: Essays on the rhetoric and poetics of the law*. Madison: University of Wisconsin Press.

Winsor, D. (1996). *Writing like an engineer: A rhetorical education*. Mahwah, NJ: Lawrence Erlbaum Associates.

Zappen, J. P. (1975). Francis Bacon and the rhetoric of science. *College Composition and Communication*, *26*, 244–247.

Zappen, J. P. (1979). Science and rhetoric from Bacon to Hobbes: Responses to the problem of eloquence. In R. L. Brown, Jr. & M. Steinmann, Jr. (Eds.), *Rhetoric 78: Proceedings of theory of rhetoric: An interdisciplinary conference* (pp. 399–419). Minneapolis: University of Minnesota Center for Advanced Studies in Language, Style, and Literary Theory.

Zappen, J. P. (1983). A rhetoric for research in sciences and technologies. In P. Anderson, R. J. Brockmann & C. Miller (Eds.), *New essays in technical and scientific communication: Research, theory, and practice* (pp. 123–138). Farmingdale, NY: Baywood.

Zappen, J. P. (1985). Writing the introduction to a research paper: An assessment of alternatives. *The Technical Writing Teacher*, *12*, 93–101.

Zappen, J. P. (1987). Historical studies in the rhetoric of science and technology. *The Technical Writing Teacher*, *14*, 285–298.

Zappen, J. P. (1989). Francis Bacon and the historiography of scientific rhetoric. *Philosophy and Rhetoric*, *8*, 74–88.

Zappen, J. P. (1991). Scientific rhetoric in the nineteenth and early twentieth centuries: Herbert Spencer, Thomas H. Huxley, and John Dewey. In C. Bazerman & J. Paradis (Eds.), *Textual dynamics of the professions: Historical and contemporary studies of writing in professional communities* (pp. 145–167). Madison: University of Wisconsin Press.

Zuckerman, H. A. (1978). Theory choice and problem choice in science. In J. Gaston (Ed.), *Sociology of science* (pp. 65–95). San Francisco: Jossey-Bass.

Author Index

Subject Index

A

Activity theory, 83-84, *see also* Cognitive apprenticeship, Situated learning

Actor network theory, 33, 64

Audience, *see also* Audience analysis
  abstract conceptions of, 10, 47, 50, 81
  as active interpreters of texts, 55, 64-65, 74, 80, 82
  centrality of in rhetoric, *xiii*
  complexity of, *xiii-xiv, xviii*, 14, 49-51, 128-129
  cooperative interaction with, *xvii*, 65, 129
  disagreements with, 12, 66, 71-72, 74-76, 78-80
  domination views of, *xvii-xix*, 8-11, 65, 127, 129-130
  dynamic character of, *xiii-xiv, xviii*, 14, 39-40, 50, 81, 106, 123-125, 127-128
  feedback and input from, 39, 46, 54-56, 58-62, 64, 66-76, 78-80, 115-118, *see also* Audience analysis, interaction
  imagined or implied, *xiii-xiv*, 10, 22, 41, 50-51, 53, 64, 128
  as participants in text production, 13-14, 105-106, 109-112, 122-125, 127
  persuading, 23, 35, 50, 63-64, 65, 69-71, 77-79, 81-82, 86-89, 91, 127-129
  familiar versus unfamiliar, 26-32, 33, 41-43, 62
  from the perspectives of authors, *xiii*, 10, 53, 64-65, 127
  as real people, *xiii*, 50-51, 53, 80-81, 128
  rhetorical perspectives of in science, 7-11
  role of knowledge about in helping authors construct arguments, 37, 39-41, 47, 117-118, 128-129
  static and passive conceptions of, *xvii*, 55, 65, 81, 127

Audience analysis, *see also* Audience
  complex nature of, 12, 56, 129
  dynamic conceptions of, 36, 128
  experienced scientists' approach to, 35, 39-43, 87-88, 91, 93-94
  gradual and ongoing character of, *xvii-xviii*, 11-12, 14, 35-36, 42, 49-51, 52, 54-56, 81, 94-95, 129
  importance of in persuasion, 12, 42-43
  interaction and, *xiv-xv, xvii-xix*, 8, 10-12, 22, 35-37, 39-51, 54-55, 80-81, 94, 105-110, 115, 127-130, *see also* Audience, feedback and input from
  model for, 12, 35-36, 44-45, 128
  qualifications of, 36, 51, 128-129
  shortcuts and tradeoffs in, 44, 51, 128-129
  strategies for, 12, 43
  category membership, 46-47
  closed-circuit television, 44-45
  generalizing from particular individuals, 45-46
  reading the literature, 43-44, 52
  social immersion, *xiv*, 36, 40, 47-49, 51-52, 129
  soliciting input from actual audience members, *see* Audience, feedback and input from
  students' experiences with, 13, 35-39, 52, 83, 85-86, 88-91, 94, *101, 104*
  for talks, 39
  types of information needed in, *51*
  vessel approach to, 39

Authorship, *see also* Scientific papers, Scientific writing
  and credit, 109, 117-119
  determining, 109, 113, 117-119
  ordering, 119-121

B

Biological simulations, *see* Simulations

Biopolymers, 60-61

Brookhaven National Laboratory, 4

C

Carnegie Mellon University, 3, 4, *20*, 38, 55

Cern particle accelerator, 7

139

www.ingramcontent.com/pod-product-compliance
Ingram Content Group UK Ltd.
Pitfield, Milton Keynes, MK11 3LW, UK
UKHW020429010325
455677UK00029B/1067